CIRCUS of SO

How I Discovered That we are All Freaks Passing as Normal

By Dawn Prince-Hughes

Circus of Souls: How I discovered we are All Freaks Passing as Normal

ISBN: 1484114620

ISBN-13: 9781484114629

Photo credits:

Cover photo, Krao Farini, Tocci Brothers, Madame Clofullia, George Williams, and the Leopard Man all used with permission from the Charles Eisenmann collection. Grace McDaniels, Aden Mummy, and Giant and Little Person all used with permission from the Syracuse University Collection.

Also by the Author

Songs of the Gorilla Nation: My Journey through Autism

Expecting Teryk: An Exceptional Path to Parenthood

Aquamarine Blue 5: Personal Stories of College Students with Autism

Gorillas among Us: A Primate Ethnographer's Book of Days

The Archetype of the Ape-man

Adam: In Touch with Ancient Ancestors

Praise for Dawn Prince-Hughes' Writing

"Dawn Prince-Hughes knows only too well the harsh burden of suffering without taxonomy, of feeling that you don't fit your fate and you don't know why or who or what gnostic Merck Manual might define your despair, as she explains in this unsettling, lyrical... ultimately redemptive memoir. [Prince-Hughes' writing is] Hildegard of Bingen by way of Jane Eyre."

New York Times Book Review

"An affecting, thoughtful memoir...delightfully quixotic and terribly sad...In print [Prince-Hughes] finds touching eloquence and clarity."

Publishers Weekly

"A revealing, first-person account in which [Prince-Hughes] opens a window...to provide an unforgettable view."

Kirkus Reviews

"Prince-Hughes [possesses] primal wisdom."

People Magazine

"In print [Prince-Hughes] finds touching eloquence and clarity....The reader will feel what the author is feeling...An excellent addition to any library's collection."

Booklist

“In this beautifully written and passionate memoir, [Dawn Prince-Hughes] takes us to the heart of what it means to be connected to all the inhabitants of this great and varied world we live in. I urge you to read this book.”

Dr. Francine Patterson, President and Founder of the Gorilla Foundation, author of Koko's Story

“Dawn Prince-Hughes is an extraordinary researcher. By turns opinionated and descriptive, quirky and authoritative, Prince-Hughes draws us into a ...consideration of our own culture. Readers will learn something new on every page of this poignant story...”

Goodreads

“Dr. Prince-Hughes offers a remarkable perspective and powerful voice...”

Rutgers University Review

“Prince-Hughes is a great writer -- and an inspiration for anyone searching for a voice.”

Seattle Magazine

“Moving...”
National Public Radio

“I have read [this] astonishing book with great admiration and delight. It is deeply moving, rings deep and true on every page and opens up [many] fundamental questions...[I]t is, above all, the very particular and personal story [she] tells which seizes one...[Prince-Hughes], I feel, understands the [archaic] mind as well as anyone on the planet, and through a sort of co-naturality or communion, no less than scientific observation. Thank you for your remarkable and candid book.”

Oliver Sacks

“A passionate memoir...[Prince-Hughes writing is] a primer on self-preservation and love.”

O Magazine

“[Prince-Hughes' writing] delights the mind and touches the heart...her obvious love [is what] makes this book so special...Prince-Hughes has written a book that speaks to our hearts and enlists our sympathies. Thank you...”

Jane Goodall

“I read [Dawn Prince-Hughes' book] with fascination and great pleasure...I found it impossible to put down...beautifully written...Not only is [her] personal story enthralling, but the insights [she] gives to readers can help anyone who has the will to pay attention. I kept thinking about it for days afterward and have since recommended it to several people.”

Jean Auel, author of the Clan of the Cave Bear series

“[W]hat a fine job [Dawn Prince-Hughes] has done…Wonderful! I deeply appreciate [this] book...”

Ray Bradbury

For Rhys

Table of Contents

Acknowledgements: Rations for the Roustabouts

"Roustabout" was a term used in the old carnival days, referring to the faceless masses of circus folks – "carnies" -- wandering, dispossessed, underpaid "muscle" that toted the water, fed the animals, pounded in stakes, raised the Big Top, and completed an unending list of other menial tasks for little thanks. In writing this book I have come to think of most of us, as we simply try to get through life, as such roustabouts. It is from this viewpoint that I thank my friends, colleagues, and family – roustabouts all – for what they have done to make the peculiar carnival of this book come to fruition. I have the pleasure of being able to thank many of the same people I have thanked in my other works since they are still in my life, to my personal and professional benefit. My son, Teryk, remains the best reason to leave a written trail in this world. My parents, Ron and Joyce, my sister Davina and brother-in-law Gregg, and my brother David Frazier also fit this description, as do my extended family and friends: Tammy Benson and family, Katherine Graves, Carol, Rusty, Nana and the girls, Shaye Areheart, the Eddings Clan, Joan, Alex, and Molly Ware, Carrie Small and family, the Dunkel family, and so many others, also mentioned elsewhere in this book. A special thanks to my agent for almost a decade, Jenny Bent.

I have appreciated the comments and insights of interesting new friends throughout the re-seeing of this work as it changed over its final stages, when even small comments made a big difference: thank you Peter Gabriel, (the late) Steve Woodruff, Michael Lieber, Oliver Sacks, Kate Edgar, and a big thank you to my friend Suzanne Paola. I would also like to thanks Random House for their six-figure investment in this work and for their generous offer to return the rights to me when I felt that I could do a better job on it than they. I thank Peter Guzzardi, who edited this work and brought the same critical eye to it that he has lent to the works of Deepak Chopra, Stephen Hawking, and other gifted writers, and to books such as The Hitchhiker's Guide to the Galaxy and The Salmon of Doubt. He helped to shape this book into a more coherent Side Show.

I extend a special thanks to Rhys Prince, who literally saved my life, who is the other half of my soul and the love of my life, and to whom this book is dedicated. Neither of us will go to the circus alone ever again.

I thank the museums listed in the pages of this work, for the exhibits that mirrored those who circled their halls, arranging their collections in such a way that those of us within them were compelled to see each other as much as we saw the displays.

I would also like to thank the museums I still dream of visiting: The Time Museum (in Rockford, Illinois), which chronicles the history of time-keeping (the exhibits are, of course, arranged in chronological order); the American Sanitary Plumbing Museum (in Worcester, Massachusetts), which plumbs the history of indoor toilets from mid-19th Century to the present (the proprietor, B. J. Manoog, regularly attends toilet bowl symposia to keep abreast of toileting trends); The Tragedy in U.S. History Museum (in St Augustine, Florida), which displays the car Lee Harvey Oswald drove to the Kennedy assassination and autopsy photos of Bonnie and Clyde, complete with bare breasts and blood rivulets running in every direction; the Museum of Menstruation (located in Hyattsville, Maryland) -- aptly anagrammed "MOM," the museum features antique pads and belts and sexy Kotex ads featuring

Lee Miller from the 1920s; the Madison Museum of Bathroom Tissue (in Madison, Wisconsin), where the museum is on a roll with samples of toilet paper from Churchill Downs, Ellis Island, the Vatican, the Alamo, and the Statue of Liberty; and in their inimitable "history of toilet paper" exhibit the museum displays grass, leaves, sand, and catalog paper. All these places keep the spirit of the Side Show alive.

Finally, I pause to pay homage here to all freakish animals of all times and places. You know who you are.

Introduction:

Passing Freaks

It is a fact that if all the Barbie dolls ever made since 1959 were placed head to toe, they would circle the earth seven times. Perhaps it is testament to the human capability to hold a perfect image in our collective minds, to strive to be that thing no matter how flawed we ourselves might be, no matter how flawed the ideal itself might be, floating in the clouds, circling the earth, the third ring for the freak show below.

I imagine a farther eye looking down on the earth, seeing the lights huddled together for strength in the passing dark, seeing the impassable Great Wall, seeing our ring of Barbies. I wonder if this farther eye would see us, trying so hard to pass through impassable walls in a deeper night; would it see the ways we all try to pass as things that we are not?

Passing strange, we pass for whole, we pass for bright, we pass for rich and beautiful in our fashion; we pass for immortal, even as our lives pass us by. *Illusion is the first of all pleasures*, Oscar Wilde said. Perhaps a farther eye sees through us, sees us all as broken animals —as freaks.

I was born an animal, perhaps the way we all were, perhaps with an earthier mind, a quicker heart. I was also born with a mountain of sensitivities, the kind they now call autism. People are surprised when I tell them that I have been diagnosed as autistic, because when they hear that word, they have in their minds a kind of black picture, a smothering and oppressive picture. Perhaps it is a fragmented picture, an old picture with the corners torn away, a picture with the shadows of the Rain Man, or developed in the dark, positive images of negatives they've seen, the upsetting black and white of words on pages. When they see me, they are surprised that I am present, that I understand them; that my eyes meet theirs, that I remain gentle. Many people have never learned that being autistic is simply being human -- but without the skin.

When most people think of autism they think of violent, unreachable people in worlds of their own making, worlds without keys. They imagine people who feel no empathy, people who lack imagination, and are unavailable to the deepest human needs for contact and love – like those children found in the woods, raised by wolves. I acknowledge that the phenomena of autism can cause great pain, both to those who have it and those who live with those who have it. But there is beauty in my way of being.

Since I was born I have felt the breath of butterflies and felt the turning of the heavens. I have bent from the weight of the breathed air and have, at times, covered my eyes to shield myself from the burning beauty of other people's eyes -- so full of wonder and regret. I have always felt everything; the too bright sun, the deafening loudness of whispers. I can taste sound and smell colors. I was and am completely permeable.

I wasn't ever able to fit into the passing puzzle of everyday life and so I left school and home at a young age, and lived on the streets. I couldn't pass as a normal person, even if the definition of "normal" during adolescence is necessarily broad, given the constant anxiety, lack of personal integration, and, among most girls my age, the pathological desire to be one of those Barbies circling the earth.

Far from being the already-molded plastic model that I was expected to be, I was rough at the edges, unwilling to be fully formed as a single, living thing. Perhaps the deep liquid that was me turned out be a sort of mirror. People didn't like what they saw. My unfocused stare, my inattention to the trends, so important; the ways I played with dogs instead of people at recess; the way I quoted Kant when asked simple questions. I would respond to taunts and then slaps and kicks by offering long-winded monologues on the philosophical reasons that violence wasn't a morally sustainable practice. I have a funny image, now that I am far away from that time and place, of Barbie and Ken roaming the toy boxes after dark, seeking the softness and weakness of weirder toys, kicking ass. Such is childhood for so many of us.

I would ignore what I thought of as the "hard people" then. I got to the point that they simply didn't exist for me. When they threw my books at me I would simply pick them up and read where the pages had been opened, looking for oracles. When they spit on me, I studied the image of water molecule models in my mind. Like rain. Like rain.

They would scream that I was a freak. When I think of the word "freak," deep in my mind -- silently, as we often do -- I see the beginning letter as a growing trunk, a foundation from which the word flows, both in the reality of a growing forest and in the linear writing of the word. The second letter stands for the branches of the tree growing on the page, and the next two letters, in their roundness with stems, become the fruit of the word. Frea…Free.

I think of the liberation of difference, of running naked and wild in the old garden before we knew we were monsters, before the end, when the harsh "k" sound that ends the word "freak" kicked us out, contained us, confined, caught in our disabilities. When they screamed that I was a freak, I would remember the kicking freedom of the word, growing my own fruits. Eventually, the words, the rain, the fruit, were not enough. My spirit was dying; I could hear it withering dry brown every day. It was logical to leave.

I remember going down to the highway from my parents' house, a mile walk by thirsty gravel from our home's front door, hitching up my fear and my second sight and hitching a ride miles down the road, a one-woman show. I was homeless for most of five years after that. I couldn't look at people properly, nor could I find my way on a map. Human Services might have been an interesting idea I read in a phone book in a cold booth on the street; but I would close a book like that, not knowing where to start because I saw the grain of the page, the busy look of the ads, smelling the ink and dirt of it, tasting where people had licked their fingers to turn the pages. I would put it down and walk away to wash my mind.

Probably I would have just washed my mind and put miles behind me until I died. But in my young adulthood, I was lucky enough to stumble upon a family of captive gorillas in a Seattle zoo. I had started working as an erotic dancer – become a worker in the sex industry. "Industry" is such a good term for that life. There is nothing natural about it -- the lights, the scraping physicality, the gears that grind and grind. I had always found my solace in nature, and with one of my first paychecks from the strip club I fought my panic at passing along the city streets and boarded a bus to the park where the zoo lived. It was when I turned a corner and saw the slow, solid gorillas, that I knew I'd found creatures who would instinctively understand me, and who I knew I would understand. They contained a way to a deeper solace, a way to settling.

I had never known real peace until I met the gorillas. The world had always moved at slicing light speed around my slowness, my plodding permeability. When I saw the gorillas for the first time, it was as if the whole world – the world that normal people take for granted and see each day with a sight also taken for granted -- had slowed to a pace I could comprehend. I went back to the zoo every chance I could, sitting silently with the gorillas, taking in their blessed predictability, the soulful scrutiny of their un-gazing. My heart slowed, finally.

I never told anyone that I was going to watch the gorillas; it was my secret. And for a long time it was only about secrets and sitting; it was as if I were going there to take deep and hidden breaths days apart and deeper each time, taking everything in and letting everything out in a rhythm as ancient and as timeless as breathing itself. I sat inside the shelter that connected with the gorillas' own, separating the loud and unseeing public from their tiny world. Then, being a freak, having my differences, was a good thing once again, as it had been at the beginning, before I knew better.

I had known this pride of porousness as a child. I had lost its peaceful kind of protection when I entered the world of human beings outside my family. Now I knew once more that my kind of sensing, my freakish feeling, was shared by other living things, like the grounded gorillas I had gotten to know. The wonder of knowing so many secret sensations was mine again.

I became aware of the comings and goings of birds and insects and night footprints, growing and falling leaves, all telling a story on the parchment of the red dust of that ground. There was a silence that came to live there when the shouting and staring people stayed away, giving over to older, quieter things that sought to reclaim their home -- like me, making paths between glass and gorilla. In this quiet sleepiness I began to wake up. I stretched and yawned in the soul I had forgotten, and the waking took months and years. I awoke a little more each spring and found rest for my weariness with each enfolding winter. I shed my multicolored armor each fall. I was lucid in this dream. I opened my eyes. I opened. I could see things anew, and I saw how alike the gorillas and I were, how like the Gorilla Nation was to the Human Nation of my birth.

I was becoming a social animal, full of empathy I had always had, nursing a preoccupation with patterns broad and rituals meaningful. I remembered how to be in an older way. Instead of the newer and narrower rituals of niceness that people offer, so fast and forgettable, my offerings were like the patterns of ancient dances. Saying "hello" would take me an hour. Saying goodbye would take a great long time, full of "hellos" prayed and remembered. Just to look in the gorillas' eyes for a moment would compel me to remember, as if counting beads on a rosary. In return I saw the rosary in their gaze. Forever. Forever.

Sometimes I was filled with joy, and wanted to shout, "There are other real and gentle people among us! Humanity is not alone! Look! Look!"

To me, this was a simply joyous story, just one of a million daily miracles that no one sees. I went on with my life, succeeding in the ways the gorillas had taught me. After watching them for years I saw all the small and common ways that people bond together to share a life. I saw the gorillas comfort each other when they were sad and full of care. I saw them smile and laugh, tickling each other with fingers and free antics, laughing. I saw them stop anger, coming forward to stop fights. There was a clear connection, the silent sincerity of the love between mother and daughter, between grandfather and other -- a spoken love in the quiet of no words, whispered by closeness alone.

I learned these ways of body and intention from the gorillas and slowly started to act them out, like a timeless play, and in doing so regained my humanity. I never rushed listening, and sat square with human beings; I knew from watching the gorillas how to comfort them with a warm arm, a held hand. I memorized the dreams and their fears of the people I met. I was quietly near them, going through the forests, human made, of forgiven failures, of laughable moments, of longing to do good in ways that were important. I told people I loved them. I went to university, I studied hard and earned a Ph.D. in anthropology, and started a family. As I lost people and dreams and fears along the way, new people gave me new dreams – and soothed new fears. It was just a life, a life beautiful and invisible, the way most lives are.

Still, I was different, and though now people knew me better and longer, they knew me in ways deep enough to tell me I was not like them. I wanted to know why. When I discovered that I qualified for a diagnosis of autism, this, too, slipped gently into a layer of my silent life, a layer of explanation between regret and small triumph. But then someone heard my story. They saw it as big, something to shout about: It was important, they said, to share it. There could be so many people like me out there, people I could help, if only I would tell it all.

My mother used to say I had a mission. She said that I had things to pass on to others. My mind used to work on this, and the word "mission" became something of what it sounds like, the hiss of a fuse, a tension, something missed in the beginning, a silent explosion, after which one must move on. Mission: for me, it all goes together, the missing, hissing, the finishing, and then the going on. Sometimes when my mother would say this word I would run outside and look up at the sky. I would meditate on other words, pushing "mission" away. There was too much tension in it.

As an adult I had often wondered where my own mission was, the one my mother spoke of so often. It seemed I was always behind it, chasing it; I had the sense that I had stumbled, maybe even in the womb, and had to race with all my might to catch up to it, my own far and dark horizon ready to explode without me. I felt that my friends could be right – sharing my story with the world, with written words, would be my mission. With my heart in the right place, where it always was, I wrote my story down. That story became my first book, *Songs of the Gorilla Nation: My Journey through Autism.*

The awareness of autism as a phenomenon is growing every day and when my new literary agent sent my manuscript around, there were nine publishing houses interested in buying it. I started to get a growing queasy feeling, like I had just gotten on a carnival ride and suddenly knew, in that animal way, that it was going to be too much, too little under my control, even before the ride started. An amusement ride with a one way ticket.

We often know it's too late like that, but instead of demanding to be let off the ride we hold on tight over the sweat, and pray we don't embarrass ourselves. I am no exception. I was scared that people would never really see my heart, and they would think everything about me was in the wrong place. I wouldn't be a healer or a hero; when people heard me, they would only hear eerie screams behind a still story. They would want to touch me to feel my fear, growing too many arms, too many weighted legs. On display, I would no longer be free, perched in the branches of freak, eating its fruit, kicking for freedom. I would be a tamed monster and everyone would know I was trying to pass as normal, alone.

Passing Strange

"She was afraid of all freaks, for it seemed to her that they had looked at her in a secret way and tried to connect their eyes with hers, as though to say: we know you. We are you!"

A description of Frankie, Carson McCuller's Heroine in The Member of the Wedding

"Every country gets the circus it deserves".

Erica Jong

The public display of freaks, of what we might think of as tamed human monsters, has a long history. It occurred to me as I prepared to meet the public that the book tour for *Songs of the Gorilla Nation* would be a kind of travelling freak show, a kind of squeaking carnival crawling through large and small towns full of normal people with all their parts in the right places. But though I feared becoming the thing in the dark, a thing of delicate and monstrous freakishness, I also felt like I wanted to tell the story of the things without voices, the misshapen souls that stared from silent tents down silent roads to more stares. I wanted to be part of history, even this kind. Though it could be a difficult history to bear, it has the comfort of ancient roots.

Hybrid and misshapen figures were painted on cave walls in the Stone Age. Clay tablets at Nineveh in Assyria illuminate no less than 62 types of bodily deformations. Ancient Egyptians depicted humans with animal heads or bodies in their pantheistic art, and Empedocles and Democritus wrote about abnormal beings to capture the imagination. In a living world not yet made machine, freaks were sacred. Whether they were considered those in whom God had taken a special interest, or as warnings of God's displeasure, they occupied the realms of heaven and hell, a kind of joining of all things between. Freaks had to be noticed, to be gazed at with respect for a God ever forming and reforming us and reforming nature, in which anything could happen. In this place the earth was animated, people were animals, and all things elemental could be shaped together like clay, fired in both difference and sameness, creations of holy whim, half-human and half-beast, caught in the middle of time and sin.

Unusual people were exhibited throughout the Dark Ages, signs and portents in a time when a visible God was still alive -- a natural paradox without the discrete trinity of distance, distance, distance.

As Certain Christian sensibilities hardened to stone, what had, in ages past, been seen more as Wondrous Births -- births that fused human and animal -- became clearer punishments of a God who no longer blessed contradiction. Wondrous births were replaced by monstrous births, caused, they said, by the unnatural sexual union between man and animal, too great a quantity of semen, too small a quantity of semen, too small a womb, the artifice of wandering beggars.

Perhaps the mother of a freakish child had seen a bear, or a lion, or some hideous sight – "maternal impression," they called it. There was another cause of the birth of the unusual: imagination itself was teratogenic, or "monster making." Not only trauma, but thinking and dreaming made monsters. Nature and the animal landscape within and without brought magic to form.

As technology took over and humans were the shapers rather than the shaped, the movements of people brought about an estrangement from the land in a flight to cities filled with the freakish – fearful travels, misshapen experiences and people wearing masks, whether grotesque or kind. Throughout the Industrial Revolution and the turn of our last century, one of our collective hairy and misshapen feet stayed in the dirt, where it could remember and grow inward, while the other stepped clean into the future. It is no accident that the freak show as we know it saw its genesis in the 19th Century, when more people were abandoning their close ties to the land and seeking the separateness of city life. As people cut themselves from the land and its creatures, they left a bright brown wound, open and un-healing, seeking a salve. The freak show drew people's wild hearts home. *Wild places*, it whispered. *"Alligator Man. Bird Woman. Dog-Faced Boy."*

Then, as now, the freak show gave us back our archaic past, nature rendered with the holy hand of creativity, our own wild shadows looking back at us, calling us home.

In the beginning of the freak show years, during the 1800s, proprietors needed only advertise that they had something to offer "To the Curious" to draw people in. The people and animals they showed were called "living curiosities." The "Ten in One," they called the shows – and you got a lot of freaks for your money. But the freakish had, indeed, lost some of the creative magic we longed for over time. Freaks became stamped-out factory models of what humans shouldn't be. The freaks were casts of sickness, pathetic and powerless, to be pitied and studied.

During the height of the display of the curious, doctors and experts were often invited to the shadowed tents of the carnival to look upon the anomalous twists of the human body for free. Their comments on the authenticity of freaks and their mysteries made great advertising copy. It was these same market spokespersons who eventually led to the decline and demise of the sideshows of the nineteenth- and twentieth -centuries, after the heyday of the freak show in America, which spanned the years from 1840 to 1940. Toward the middle of the twentieth century, what made freaks "freaks" became medicalized. "We know what it is," the experts said, "we know what causes different skin, different bodies, and different brains."

The anomalous twistings of humanity were no longer a mystery: they were the result of a dizzying list of diseases. The early twentieth century saw the emergence of genetics in the black, yellow and green of Gregor Mendel's peas, a man of God who gave us the final end of a certain kind of faith. Darwin's champions cried survival of the fittest, and in their fits warned that if we harbored and nurtured misshapen people, the people whose minds swirled, if we hold to our breast the imperfect, the misfit, the weak, we would surely see our demise. The bizarre should not breed. The flawed should not flourish.

Hormones and X-rays, smeared and shot, began to reveale the mechanisms of monstrosity. Human differences became pathological, and singularity became sickness. In 1937, *Colliers* magazine told us in an article titled "Side Show Diagnosis" that "…all side show freaks…could be fitted snugly between the pages of some medical textbook. Curiosities they may be, but what they more certainly are is sick."

The great divide, we pretended. We were free, we pretended, and they -- always they -- were safely put away, amputated from us, their teeth pried loose from our thighs. In my mind's eye I imagine a man in a pristine smock, wearing a pale and practiced expression of concern, dutifully taking the temperature of the Lizard Boy. "Turn your head and cough," he says, turning aside and clearing his own throat.

As decent people averted their eyes from malignancy, disability became pornography and freak shows shut down, because what was behind the new statements of origin, what was at first unsaid, was "*we can fix it*." Human oddities were taken from the road and incarcerated in institutions, some of which employed such "therapeutic" devices as the Lunatic Box, a coffin-like case in which a patient, the living dead, was forced to stand in his or her own excrement and sleep bent at the knees. The same institutions employed metal strait jackets, dunking tubs, immobilizing chairs where patients were tied for up to six months, fever cabinets and restraint cages trapping and choking, trying to tame them, trying to free the freak from itself. These institutions drew no line between physical and mental impairment. They took anyone, adding to their own freak show, one thriving behind brick walls and whispers.

But because our need to see a reflection of our own damaged souls persists, the freak show itself is still very much alive. Now the modern media, like the dime museum lecturers and carnival barkers before them, keep the show moving.

This was the world I was prepared to enter as a freak writing about itself -- this modern carnival circuit -- to be put in a habitat somewhere in the light of television, *The Gorilla Girl* just the latest in the streaming torrent of gratuitous show titles: *The He/Shes Who Sleep with Straight Men; You're Too Fat for the Beach; Stop Acting Like a Member of a Different Race; Twins with Different Sexual Preferences; May/December Romances.*

Fifty years after the inauguration of the tabloid press, it has become difficult to distinguish between the so-called legitimate press and the carnival press, not only in newspapers and magazines, but also in book publishing. There are tell-all biographies, personal histories of abnormality of one kind or another, and memoirs, like mine, of individuals *in extremis*.

The literature of the old sideshow is not gone, just reborn. The long-gone "True Life" booklets of the Golden Age of the Freak Show, such as *the Life and History of Alfonso, the Human Ostrich*; *Interesting Facts and Illustrations of the Royal Padaung Giraffe-Neck Women*; or *Personal Facts Regarding Percilla the Monkey Girl* are now replaced by the well-publicized books of the legitimate press, the author primed for the circus circuit, to stand and speak on the stage, to turn and return into the camera's light, to stop in the dust of every town in the country, the object of rapt gaze.

I fought the feeling that people who came to hear me, or who saw me in the press, would only be showing up for a sideshow, to see if my face looked different, if my body moved in some frightening but hypnotizing way, to see from the safety of a crowd, if I would speak strangely, or rock and gibber.

Many times before my publicity tour, in the dead of night, I would be convinced that the imp of the perverse would take me in some horrible way as I stood in front of hundreds of people, and I would start to do these things, employing my repertoire of gorilla sounds and private delight in jumping on furniture. In my mind's eye, I saw people, having hurried to the book signing from their PTA meetings, suddenly scattering in my wake, proper handbags flying and ties flapping. They would be horrified as I swung and leaped from podium to folding chair, my own torn book in my mouth, my eyes wild.

Once I read about a circus act in which a box of illusion turned an ordinary woman into a gorilla. The audience's minds reeled as they moved in closer, trying to see what was real and what was illusion, their curiosity pulled them in. They couldn't stop looking. Their experience was what Freud called "that class of frightening which leads back to what is known of old and long familiar."

Maybe I would be their missing link…a link back to something they were, something they lost. That is what I prayed. I didn't believe it.

The Gorilla Girl

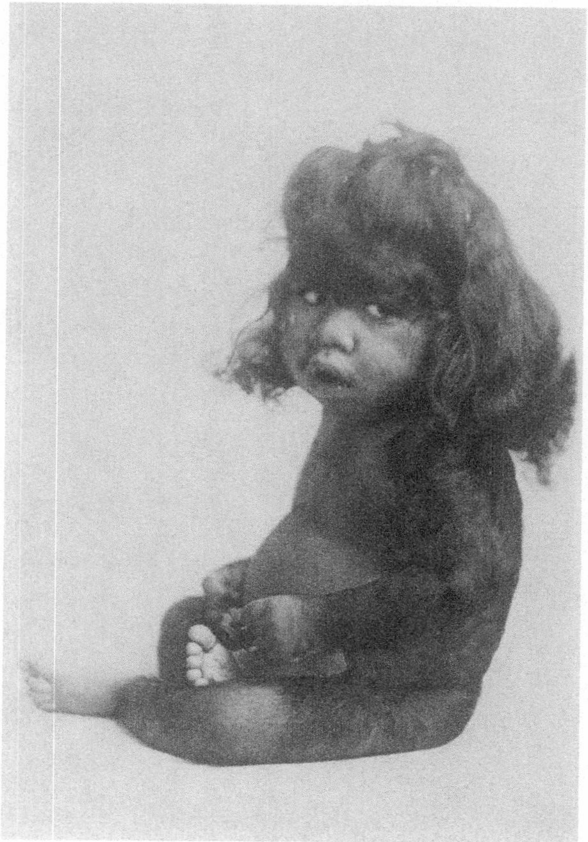

And The Circus of Loneliness

"Her pupils are sparkling and dark black, hair covers her head and reaches far down her back, hair covers her body from head to feet..."

So goes a description of Barnum's original missing link, Krao Farini, a young child taken from Thailand in the early 1800s for display in America. He tells us that she looks like a gorilla. She was called "The Ape Woman." She was, the Circus Master said, the Missing Link.

She was exhibited naked, for people wanted to know if she was a "person." In a picture I have, Krao, the child, sits unclothed, malleable and primate, the light skin and dark hair of her body a contrast to the man on whose lap she sits. In a heavy, dark, Victorian suit with buttons up to the neck, he gives nothing away. The small girl on his lap stares out, maybe a person, maybe not.

The fact that Krao spoke several languages and was very well-read was not discussed by her promoters. She died in New York in 1926, at age 49, not that much older than I am.

That is what I will be, I thought. *I will be like The Ape Woman, or like that girl in the magic trick. I will be the Woman who tried to turn into a gorilla and got caught in the freak between. I will be naked, seen for what I am, a carnival of one. Like generations of feral children before me, I would be a Missing Link.*

Of course, even before my book came out I knew on some level that I was not a carnival of one. For one thing, my difference never lets me forget that I am a part of everything and so I am never alone in some deeper sense -- it loves me hard, and I love it hard in return. My connectedness demands my empathy. But even in terms of being freakish I knew that there were other people who had been freaks, if not exactly like me, then in ways, collectively, constructing a pastiche that made me feel whole. It was good to know that I am not alone under my particular Big Top, that some other people have experienced life as I have.

Friedrich Nietzsche, for example, battled madness all his life. One day when he saw a horse being abused by its master, he broke down in tears, tenderly throwing his arms around the horse's neck, as I would, weeping. This began a period of psychological turbulence that led to his spending the last eleven years of his life in an asylum. Gustave Flaubert, who had an unusual attachment to objects, just as I do, kept his lover's slippers and mittens in his desk drawer – the Human Pack Rat. Socially unpredictable; I once ate an entire meal with my fingers, sitting at a banquet table with Jane Goodall. I was envious when later I heard that James Russell Lowell removed and proceeded to eat with knife and fork, a bouquet of flowers from the centerpiece at a literary supper.

J.M. Barrie ordered Brussels sprouts for lunch every day but never ate them. He said he hated Brussels sprouts, but loved the words. Like me, he was moved by the persistent beauty of sounds. Henry David Thoreau listened to and talked with all the things that lived in the forest.

Perhaps all writers are odd forest people, who long to add to the persistent droning sweetness and call of the world. Going out on unseen limbs alone, we use words as song, and put song into our words, listening, and waiting, for something to come back to us.

"Human salvation lies in the hands of the creatively maladjusted," wrote Martin Luther King, in *Strength to Love*. In these readings I absorbed before my tour I began to believe that perhaps I'm not autistic at all. I'm just a writer.

I feel words. “Animal,” for instance, is a warm, slick word. In it there is a kind of smoothness that flows through animal muscles in slow motion, a kind of universal oil, a thick tea of tendon, the sweat of sinew. I stretch it out in my mind: *aannnnniiiiiimmmmaaallll.* It is a word that reminds me of a beginning to which we must always return. That is why it works its way through all that is written here about our secret stretchings and our hidden hides. It comes out in our furtive fleeing from the flaws that claw at us; it is revealed in our bare chests as we find the bravery to show what we are inside.

To me, “passing” is a hollow word. Passing as what we are not is what makes it hollow -- the hollowness of all things given up for dead. There is nothing in this word, nothing of substance, because it echoes with emptiness. The word, like the very possibility of emptiness, of not being whole, causes me discomfort. Just saying the word “passing” in my mind makes existence feel ghostly, gone.

I seek the substance and sustenance of words, and their meaning gives me shelter, a place to live. The word – and therefore the idea – of passing often runs through my mind, and I will say it over and over again, unwilling to let it go, wanting to color it or order it before I, too, pass away. And so the words “passing” and “freaks” are related in my mind; passing becomes the phantom that is left after our fear of falling, the passing of our perfection. Passing is the word that haunts the emptiness that is left when we cover up what is different about us--the colorful parts, the extra parts, the parts in the wrong place.

"Passing" is the thin gauze curtain that we throw on our naked freakishness, hiding ourselves. We cannot separate the freak from the ways we pass as normal. It makes for a kind of emptiness, loneliness. Most people would not say out loud that they are freaks passing as normal. They say it in other ways, ways that the writer, the poet, reports.

As my dance with my readers and other people I met on the way unfolded, I became intrigued by the haunting stories of difference and I began to keep a scrapbook, a picture book, a book full of black and white templates for human entanglement and damage. As I thumbed through the growing pages I found comfort in the knowing stare of the Man with Two Faces, in the hands of Johnny Eck, whose missing legs and pelvis led to his being known as the Half-Man, in Betty Lou Williams and her twin, who stuck out of her side like a baby forever in the act of being born, and in Percilla the Monkey Girl. All these pained souls and whisperers of secrets would come to finish for me what the gorillas had started. They would become the gray ghosts I saw behind each living eye.

I started to identify deeply with them, to feel as though they would be with me as I crossed the country on my carnival circuit. More than just looking out from the haunting black and white of the photographs I started collecting, they would be looking out of my eyes at a larger world, and, surprisingly, in the world looking back.

The afternoon before one of the first appearances on my book tour I went to Ripley's Believe It or Not Odditorium in San Francisco, which opened in 1939, a year before the commonly accepted death of the freak show. This was the closest I could get to the kind of reunion I longed for. The street I walked just to get there was like a stroll down the midway, but in broad daylight. There were shiny baubles and twisted manikins and every kind of imaginable stuffed animal for sale. I walked past several life-size caricatures of talking prospectors with huge noses, police and firemen with burnt red cheeks, a Buddha with an enormous belly, his eyes closed to me -- all this on street corners and shops before I even entered the Odditorium.

Once inside the Odditorium itself I saw a bust of an African woman with a padlock through her nose. The plaque told me that many women of the Djerma Tribe did this in order to imitate a historical queen, whose husband, tired of her gossiping, had put a padlock on her nose and threatened to padlock her lips if she didn't stop talking about people.

"Some people will do anything," a woman snorted, walking by in an animal skin jacket with cigarettes in the pocket.

Nearby was a life-size statue wearing furs, a headhunter. The plaque said, "Igarot man/woman." The statue had breasts and carried a spear. Apparently Igarot men and women were completely interchangeable.

In another room, a visitor fixed her makeup in the reflective surface of a display case containing a model of the head of Liu Chung, a Chinese Governor of State, born in the 900s with double pupils. A fat family stood in front of a case housing a model of the heaviest man ever drafted into the Army, Robert Earl Hughes, who was 709 pounds. Together the family and I walked on to a case with a model of Edward Hagner, the world's thinnest man at 5'7" and 48 pounds. We were all huge in comparison.

One room was full of ritual masks from different tribes. Amid the bright colors and severe carvings, the silently displayed raffia and shells, the rattles and bells, a placard explained, presumably to some kind of theoretical audience who knows nothing about hiding their identities: "a mask hides a dancer's true identity and transforms him into a different spirit, individual, or creature."

The room of masks, somehow appropriately, was attached to a fake graveyard made of Styrofoam tombstones with funny things written on them, like "Here lays an atheist. All dressed up and nowhere to go." People all dressed up with nowhere to go laughed, and passed.

The last thing I looked at was a machine that showed how different the two sides of our faces are -- how we become a completely different person if the left side of our face is made into a whole, and a wholly different person with two right sides. With two of one side of my own face I find that I am more beautiful than I am usually; the other sides put together make me uglier than I normally am. I am happy with the compromise I see in the mirror every day. I wonder what other people see as I notice that the people walking behind me seem to hover for a moment in the mirrored curves beside my image and then fall into me, disappearing into my beauty and ugliness. They become part of me, poor and rich, young and old, mixing races and time, passing behind and into, animals passing before and around me. The real museum, the real menagerie, is in our heads and on my face.

It reminded of the projector Athanasius Kircher built in the 1600s. Using the angles of mirrors or curved glass or colored crystals, you could see yourself "as a crane-necked man…the horn of a rhino growing from your head," or be a goat, or ugly, or horned, or wrinkled. A man could see himself as a woman, or a woman as a man. The crystals could make your skin "red like satyrs, yellow like jaundice, blue or black like Ethiopians." The machine also used a wheel of mirrors on which the heads of animals were painted.

Kircher said, "There are a thousand ways to deform a man…no monster is so ugly whose shape you will not find in yourself."

This is the most important thing I would come to know during my book tour: the ways we are deformed and pulled out of shape, the ways we are cut apart, but pass as whole. Throughout the rest of my tour I learned of the surprising tenderness of the humanity around me and the awareness of most people that they are flawed, that they are freakish, so worthy of display and yet so hidden, part animal and part magus. I know now that we each struggle with our freakishness, obvious yet shared secretly with the other clowns, the other legless wonders, the fire-eaters, the contortionists, the other freaks born and made.

As I traveled across the land, the story of my freakishness became a bigger story, our story, the human story; and now the stories of the people I met have become mine; stories of fellow passengers sad and grotesque under beautiful faces, people missing parts of themselves and laughing in joy beside the mirror. It is a history, a *lusus naturae* of our collective reflections. There is no way to keep "freaks" from being "us." They are not the other, they never were; they are our deepest selves.

As we sit on the midway, stuffed animals with glassy eyes, waiting to be won, there is something nagging at us, a certain familiar strain of music, a calliope whistling to us from the distant outposts of the human frontier, to those more twisted and sculpted, more strained and stretched. "Nothing is too strange to be a part of you…" it says, "for you yourself are passing strange."

I believe now that when we shut the human animals away, shut down our monsters and make them disappear, we become half of what we were meant to be. The carnival, the circus, the Side Show, continues in our minds, behind our eyes. We need the show. We know, secretly, that we all belong in it.

In this book I have written about that familiarizing journey -- of seeing the freakish as normal and the normal as freakish. Like the old photographs in my book of freaks, the freaks themselves become normal, metaphors for the ways we are all damaged, painted from within and without.

I have seen that there are things we should pick up, and things we should put down, tired from the load. I have seen that we feel the loss of each other as we move far and fast in our culture. Now weary, we want to hear the story of our own strangeness, not in passing, but in some way that is a strong rattling thing of string and chains that holds us together, links us to other people. And as I look out on a strange world, I see that apart, we are too loose; our common strangeness ties us as we pass as normal: passing for, passing through, passing on. So my mind says.

Here I have tried to weave a history of our own display, a story in the round of what has come around again. What you have in your hand is a slice of circus, a measure of the midway, a fossil of freak show. It is a carnival with a cover. If I come to your house and pull it down from the bookshelf, I hope I will find its corners stained with dust and sugar, smelling of popcorn, smeared with the grease of the ride, your place held with a worn ticket stub.

We will never stay in one place too long on these pages, you and I. We are passing, passing all the time. There is a lot to see, so keep moving on the dirt and sparse grass under your feet, past each tent, and touch each word barked and whispered in the shadows, after the masks go down. Hurry, hurry – step right up and see the Circus of Souls.

Passing For

The Bear Woman and My Father, the Bearded Lady

Take gode hede that noon be retteyned but he be passable so that noo fawte be in his persone.

Caxton, 1489

It was late afternoon as I watched my father shaving. I call her father, but her name is Bear. Because Bear was older, because she contained me, protected me, she has become a father to me. Both bear and person, man and woman, able to germinate and gestate in one body, she was a fitting vessel for beginnings.

Bear's face was always warm, the first thing I noticed when she took me in when I was homeless. She cooked me chicken and dumplings like my mother had. Always watching out for others, she was always being watched, but Bear didn't care about being watched; she was used to it. I knew from studying people's faces when they observed Bear, that she, like others of her kind, was the strangest of the strange. If you don't even know if someone is a boy or a girl then where do you stand? It is, after all, the first announcement of our supposed normalcy.

I imagined the doctor at Bear's birth, saying with a confident and beaming smile, "It's a girl!" Wrong from the start: the story of freaks.

Sitting passively on the gritty floor of her bathroom, I stretched my legs across the old, cracked tile, thinking it was too cold in there -- worried that my father should keep warmer. The apartment was the kind she always had, namely the kind she could afford. I watched her dab her face delicately with shaving cream, her pinky held out, showing the interesting femininity that was also such a part of her. She reached for a razor and I stared, observing unselfconsciously the way she looked at herself in the mirror. She raked the razor over her soft skin, taking off the stiff hair that grew there. She had always had a beard. She sometimes shaved it off and sometimes did not. Suddenly it seemed odd that I'd never paid attention to it; it was grand and spoke for her.

So often she had given me heart, given me bearings when I was on the street. She was the first person to explain to me why people are the way they are. Her explanations stuck with me because they were loving, even if people in the street seldom loved her. I believed everything she said, despite the fact that once she broke down on a fire escape, telling me in a very convincing way that she had never known anything at all. I remember the scratching sound, the horrible roughness of those words, as she ran her callused hands over her face, pushing out tears. I thought it was amazing that someone crying so hard could stop crying so fast. Maybe that was the strength a beard could give.

I had read in history that beards had a power religion and state often sought to control. Alexander the Great thought beards made convenient handles for the enemy to use while hacking off the heads of his soldiers, so he ordered his entire army to shave. Gregory of Tours said that among the successors of Clovis it was the exclusive privilege of royalty to have long beards, a fashion that lasted until the time of Louis the Debonnaire, after which only the peasantry allowed their hair and beards to grow long in defiance.

This tradition became abhorrent to Catholic clergy over time, and toward the end of the eleventh century the pope decreed that uncut, unshaven hair was an offense to be addressed by excommunication. Supported by the ecclesiastical authorities all over Europe, the decree went even further, declaring that such persons would not even be prayed for after death. When the tide turned in favor of shaving, countless men of the court believed every manly virtue would be lost along with their beards. *Desde que no hay barba, no hay mas alma* they cried: "We have no longer souls since we have lost our beards."

I couldn't imagine Bear having no soul; it was all she was made of. But I knew her power over people was such that her beard disappeared when she spoke. It was a power I admired, because all of my life, when I spoke to people, I could see reflected in their eyes the hair I must have had growing everywhere. They say that bears are the first animal that children recognize. Maybe this stays with us.

I always thought that Bear looked like a pretty Frank Sinatra. Supposedly it was part of my disability that I don't recognize categories of people, whether men or women, one person or two. Myself, I never felt like anything, categorical or not, or maybe I felt like an angel with nothing between my legs, nothing in my bloodstream, nothing and everything on my face. I knew that people who glanced at Bear in the street probably thought she was just a man passing by. If they looked again, maybe they believed she was trying to pass as a man. Really she just wanted to pass by.

Many times I'd heard about women who wanted to pass as men, though I was never exactly sure what passing meant.

In 1688, the French essayist Jean de la Bruyere said that the perfect life would be to live as a beautiful girl from the age of thirteen to the age of twenty-two, and then become a man for the rest of your days. Apparently many women have become men and done just that.

In 1720 May Read and Ann Bonney were convicted of piracy, having swashbuckled, stolen and maimed their way across the high seas dressed in male clothing. Dr. James Barry (aka Miranda Stuart) rose to become the Inspector General of army hospitals in Britain. Deborah Sampson fought for the Fourth Massachusetts Regiment in the Revolutionary War.

The West Coast, where I lived, had long put out a halcyon call to people who wanted to pass as something or someone else. The Gold Rush had offered all kinds of unique opportunities for men and women who were like men -- perhaps *were* men. Charlie Parkhurst worked as a stagecoach driver for Wells-Fargo for twenty years and even (gasp!) voted. In the 1850s Lilly Hitchcock Hoit loved to go out dancing in men's clothes, a crime punishable in those days by prison time. Because she was wealthy, she was left alone by the police.

From the time Jeanne Bonnett was fifteen, she wore men's clothes. She got into trouble for theft, landing herself in San Francisco's first reformatory --"the Industrial School" – although an infusion of industry did little to cure Jeanne. On her release she started to organize a boys' gang for the purpose of thievery. Her illegal activities were, claimed the newspapers, "seldom equaled by even the more daring men of her class for their boldness of execution."

Many years later a small man named Jack Garland served as a lieutenant in the Spanish American War. Moving to San Francisco, he lived in boarding houses; and over the next thirty years, acted as a kind of freelance social worker. He served as a male nurse during the earthquake and fire of 1906, and provided emergency medical care for the homeless. Everyone called him Uncle Jack. After collapsing on September 18th, 1936, he was taken to a hospital. After his death it was discovered that Uncle Jack was a woman, and not just any woman, but Jeanne Bonnett. Though it could be argued that Jeanne had finally followed an industrious path, she – or he --had a dual nature to the end.

Jeanne came from wealth. It was said her mother's father was a Supreme Court Justice in Louisiana. Of her mother, Jeanne said:

"I loved my mother with all my heart. I feared even to talk to her at times, lest my rough manner might offend her. From a tomboy full of ambitions, I was made into a sad and thoughtful woman. I commenced to be rebellious. My mother feared for my future, and thought that nothing but a convent would save me, and there I remained. How I yearned for that freedom I dreamed of and how often I wished I could enjoy the liberty that the world sees fit to allow a boy."

I watched Bear gently lift her nose with her finger and make short scrapes with the razor over her still upper lip. I studied her carefully as she took the rest of the white off of her face in even strokes, making darker trails underneath the cheap cream. She had always been free in her heart, which is why no one ever felt sorry for her, sorry for her poverty, or her health. I knew she could collapse like daring Jeanne; she had a bad heart, or rather a good and free one, and therefore damaged. She told me once that she'd had a "silent heart attack." She was too proud to have a loud one. I doubted anyone would discover, as so often happened with women passing as men, her true identity after death.

My thoughts continued to dwell on the family of the freakish, on the history of him and her. The women who were said to pass as men not only dressed like men, but also voted, like Charlie Parkhurst the Wells-Fargo stagecoach driver. They passed in speech and in work, in love and soldiering, in saving and feeding, in simply living.

An American Indian woman named Cora Anderson made her way in the world as Ralph Kerwinnieo for thirteen years. I remember seeing a picture of her two selves; on the left was the image of a handsome man with dark eyes in a bowler hat and tie and suit. His generous mouth accentuated a strong, broad jaw and manly cheekbones. On the right was a more fragile-looking young woman with a smaller mouth and plump cheeks, wearing a frilled hat and modest dress, an unassuming, if sad-looking, lady in her youth. Side by side the two Ralphs, the two Coras, looked like a perfectly matched married couple. And so they were.

When discovered and arrested for "disorderly conduct" in 1914, Ralph, the perfect man seemed to speak for all women, and Cora, the perfect woman, for all men: "Do you blame me for wanting to be a man, free to live life in a man-made world? In the future centuries, it is probable that woman will be the owner of her own body and the custodian of her own soul. [But] the well-cared for woman [now] is a parasite…"

I had a friend who I suppose agreed with Cora's feelings. Whether through birth or philosophy she decided she was not a woman at all -- that her aim was not to pass as a man, but to be one. She started taking hormones, called androgynes. The first thing I noticed was that she smelled different when I hugged her. Then, over time, her beautiful face became his handsome one. I stopped calling her Bonny and started calling him Aidan. Rather than being my friend, my sister, he was now my friend, my brother.

The only time I made a pronoun mistake was when he visited me at home with his own identical twin sister, still a woman. In my mind it was like seeing some kind of odd, late night ad for a gender-changing pill: *Before. After. Before. After*. I apologized for referring to him as "she" and I ran my fingers across his smart goatee. There was a sparkle of happiness in his eyes that had never been there before. My fear all along was that something essential, soulful, about him would change, would be lost in his transition. My fears were unfounded..

I wanted to learn what my new brother had gone through, what his concerns were, what he had to think about each day. I looked up female-to-male passing tips on computer sites that gave transitioning men tips on things like shaving, or adding realistic stubble. There were instructions on how to tie a bow tie. There were resources for those who would become short men. I found advice for binding your breasts (use an Ace bandage and *lots* of Gold Bond Medicated Powder) and also products for breast binding: Enell "Bro" Binder; Underworks Binding Products; and the Loving Comfort Breast Binder from CMO Incorporated.

Most interesting were the penile prosthetics. There were tips for making a "homemade stuffer" as well as cyber skin stuffers (including the Mango Products "Packy," "The Tricky," "Mr. Softie," and the "Early to Bed Packy"). My favorite finds were the STP, or Stand To Pee stuffers, which included the Mango 2, and the Pissin' Passin' Packer.

I was surprised to find an actual medical prosthetic for men who'd lost their penises through traumatic injury. Made to look and feel real, these prosthetics were put on with special surgical glue so that a man could shower with it on, or make love. "Traumatic injury" seemed an understatement to me in this context. I wondered if my brother Aidan felt like he was born with that injury.

Bear knew Aidan, and was angry when he decided to be a man. Bear felt that it was part of the spiritual design to be what you were at birth, and didn't understand why some women felt they had to alter themselves through hormones and surgery. Bear and Aidan fought about it. Bear, like Cora/Ralph, was Native American. I wondered if that made a difference in how she viewed these things.

As I sat and watched Bear I remembered driving from Montana to Seattle many years earlier. I pulled into a row of dumpsters to pee; I needed them for cover because women can't just pee in public, even when they are in the wilderness a hundred miles from a town. I looked around with the learned awareness that women have and stepped behind one of the dumpsters. When I squatted down I realized there was a small dead bear lying beside me.

Rotting, it was melting into the ground with its claws chopped away, a hole in its side, like Christ's wound, where its gall bladder had been taken out. Its distinguishing genitals were cut away, its head severed by some sharp blade. Feeling guilty, like Longinus without a spear, I scraped together some of the hair that had fallen off its body, to bring to Bear so she could say a prayer for it.

Bear reached for a towel and wiped her face clean. When she raised her bare arms to scrub her forehead, I noticed the tattoos that had been there since I first met her, two peculiar ocean waves on the inside of her biceps. With her arms over her head, it looked as if she were emerging from some personal ocean. A bear can swim a mile and a half. I heard of one bear that swam nine miles in the Gulf of Mexico. Bear never told me what the waves meant to her. Somehow I just knew.

She leaned against the old-fashioned sink for a minute, looking into the mirror, this way and that, inspecting her face. She was a bearded lady: two of one thing, half-a-dozen-of another, as my mother would have said. Bear wasn't passing as anything. Maybe none of those other women were, either.

In the mirror, she caught me watching her.

"Let's go talk about your life," she said as she lit an American Spirit cigarette. As we walked down the hall, I followed her broad back in a trail of smells: shaving cream, smoke, and the ocean.

We sat in Bear's parlor, looking out the small window toward the ocean, which we couldn't see; but we knew it was there. In 1851 John Low, Lee Terry, and David Denny had settled here, in the place that became Seattle, named after the Indian leader of the Duwamish and Suquamish tribes. When these bearded pioneers found perfect land on the shores of the Puget Sound, they sent word to those waiting back home. "There is plenty of room for 1,000 settlers," they said. Years later, Chief Seattle's homeless granddaughter could be seen wandering the streets of the city named for her grandfather.

Bear's plain life was all around us: pens and pencils on an old table; the plastic box for her heart medicine; her reading glasses; a cup half-full of cold tea; her paintings. Each of them was simple, all dabbed-upon, unframed canvases -- straightforward at first glance, bold and clear, lined, with animals in them. I wondered if Jeanne Bonnet's boarding house room might have looked like this, and if in the end, it was any different from a room in a convent. Perhaps holiness found certain people no matter where they lived. Bear was holy.

When I started reading about bearded women I was surprised to learn of the number of women saints who were bearded: St. Galla, St. Paula, St. Liberata, was not born with a beard, we are told, but found herself being forced into marriage with a pagan despite her conversion to Christianity. She beseeched God to bless her with some affliction that would make her ugly, and God caused St. Liberata to grow a beard. After her fiancé rejected her, her furious father crucified her. Iconographers claim that this legend explains the many paintings from the Middle Ages that show a beautiful and womanly Christ.

"Well," Bear said, rolling her cigarette between her thumb and finger thoughtfully, exhaling slowly with a grunt, "You did it, Sonny. You wrote a book!"

I looked out the window through the fuzzy smoke and suddenly my focus narrowed to my own reflection in the glass. As my thoughts drifted, I looked out toward the ocean again, remembering that a sliver of moon would be rising behind us soon. On the table was my new book, and under that the scrapbook of freaks I had started working on. Sometimes Bear and I glanced at the freaks, barely visible. They were silent, as we were. I thought about the fact that bears in real life are almost always silent. In movies their sounds have to be dubbed in. For us a new story was taking shape; but as with so many things we had known together, we knew this without talking. Bear drew in a deep breath of smoke.

"Did you know that a Parker black ball-point pen has 28,000 feet of ink in it?" I asked. Bear was used to my sudden utterances of obtuse facts. She was interested in everything, so it always worked out well. I went on. "That's enough ink to draw a line from the first base camp to the summit of Mount Everest."

"Hmm," Bear grunted as she looked out the window, too. "That what you used to write your life story?"

There was a long silence as I contemplated the fact that Bear's life story was just as interesting, just as important as mine, but it would never be written down. The history behind it was too long. She would have to write about the woman Pharaoh Hatshepsut who lived in 1520 B.C., who insisted all her portraits show her with a beard. She would have to tell of the priestess of Athena, who grew a beard when her people were in danger. She would have to write about the bearded woman that Hippocrates described, in the fifth century before Christ, who grew a beard after menopause, when the ancients still believed that bearded women possessed special gifts and could be oracles of the gods.

In her life story Bear would need to write about Margaret of Parma, regent of the Netherlands in the 16th century, whose beard delighted her. She commanded her physicians to make concoctions that would make her beard grow long and soft.

Then there was Urselin (the Bear) Van Beck, who was visited by John Evelyn on September 15, 1651. Of her he had said,

"I saw the hairy woman, twenty years old, whom I had before seen when a child. Her very eyebrows were combed upwards and all her forehead as thick and even as growes on any woman's head, neatly dressed. A very long lock of hair out of each eare. She also had the most prolix beard and Mustachios…"

Bearded women with the voices of little girls, many were said to be. Their beards grew in when they were six or seven, when they started to understand the dangers of the world.

Lady Olga, a circus performer born in 1874 in North Carolina, said,

"Every woman who is lucky enough to have a beard should learn how to take care of it. Never use too hot a curling iron on the beard. It makes the hair brittle, and destroys the fine sheen." She went on to say that she "spent a week learning the secret of beard beauty culture from them, and took a postgraduate course, so to speak, in Moscow…." She instructed the bearded ladies who might heed her," Wash the beard in warm milk once a week. It keeps the lustre and color perfect…. Also, avoid eating Chinese noodles -- if you want to keep a good beard looking really nice."

I couldn't see Bear, who loved her food, avoiding Chinese noodles.

Another famous bearded lady of the 1800s was Madam Squires. According to *Brief History of a Celebrated Lady, Namely, Madam*

Squires the Bearded Lady, a booklet sold wherever she appeared, she was:

> A woman of extensive travel, great reading, and innate perceptive faculties, which give her an almost instantaneous knowledge of the human character…In disposition she is most kind and womanly, loving all and hating none. While the wonderful magnetism nature has endowed her with enables her to exercise a magic spell upon all who come within her large and varied acquaintance…she looks upon all around her, of whatever condition or religion, as her brothers and sisters, and is ready at all times to help the struggling ones on earth with a warm grasp of the hand, a kind loving word or an assuring smile.

Madame Clofullia came from Switzerland in the 1850s, adorned with jewels, the Bearded Lady of Geneva. She and her son Albert, himself covered with hair over his body, boarded the steamer *City of Manchester* and set out for Philadelphia. In New York City she was met by none other than P.T. Barnum, who sent her to a battery of doctors in order to determine that she was, indeed, a bearded lady. Doctors proclaimed that her breasts were large and fair (and strictly characteristic of the female, they added for good measure).

With her authenticity proved, Madame Clofullia received an offer from Barnum that she couldn't resist. Madame Clofullia and Albert, billed as "the Infant Esau" after the hairy son of biblical Isaac and Rebekah, made their public debut in Barnum's museum. The very first day a man hired by Barnum came to see Madame Clofullia, examining her from close and far, from this angle and that angle. Then he loudly denounced her as a fraud, a male disguised as a female. The case even went to court, although it was eventually dismissed, and the news media of the day chronicled the unfolding events every step of the way -- much to Barnum's delight, since the exhibition was filled to capacity. My mind drifted back to Bear's question.

"No, I didn't use a pen at all to tell my story." Something about that made me sad. I had typed it in, making snowless, groundless tracks as I walked over the keys, the keys of my life, without a summit to howl on.

Bear took another drag on her cigarette and then crushed it; she was trying to smoke only a little at a time these days. I thought back to the dead bear thrown away behind the trash can. I read that Asians consume a hundred tons of bear bile every year, the kind bears make in their gall bladders. They even have bear bile farms, where 10,000 bears are kept, their bile drained through surgically implanted devices. People pay more for black market gall bladders than they do for some narcotics. Bears all over the world are killed to meet that demand. I wondered if Bear's gall could cure her own hurts, her cancers, the redness of her eyes, her chronic pain.

"So what was it like?" She asked, giving me a long look. I knew she was talking about the process of selling the book.

I told Bear what it was like to go to Random House in New York, to walk into an enormous boardroom where the staff was waiting at a huge mahogany table where we would all sit, with me at the head. The staff people stood up when I came in, then waited for me to sit down. I wondered if they were anticipating I'd do something weird, or totally outrageous. After all, they had read my manuscript.

I told them: "I feel like I should be carving a turkey or something." After they all laughed, it was better.

They were nice to me, I told Bear: They said the manuscript made them cry.

"That's something," Bear admitted.

"Yeah, it is." I thought about all the manuscripts they had probably read, and how even Jesus' memoir might seem slow. I was just lucky, I guessed. I got them on a crying day.

"It was the weirdest thing, though," I told Bear. "At one point when I was sitting there talking about my story, I suddenly had this overwhelming feeling that I'd been homeless just a second ago, really hungry and pissed off; then, like magic, I was sitting in this swank boardroom with all these people, strangers who suddenly knew me better than I knew myself."

"What'd you do?" She asked.

"I felt like I was gonna start crying, but I didn't, because when I looked over at my agent, she gave me a stern, warning look that said, 'Don't do it. Don't do it no matter what.' Later she said part of the test of the meeting was to see how I handled pressure." I looked out the window for a minute and tried to remember that they all cared about me, though none of it was real.

"A couple of hours later they called my agent as I sat in my borrowed room in Manhattan watching the sunset. When she told me how much money they offered, I had to lie down in the hall. I remembered looking out the window of this place on East 74th Street, to the east, a little north, toward Brooklyn, where Coney Island was -- dancing bears, bearded ladies by the ocean. I told myself, *my life is about to become a carnival*."

"And the rest is history, huh, sweetie?" Bear smiled and lit another cigarette even though it had only been a couple minutes since she pushed the last one down and out. "You done good, son. I'm proud of you."

As our comfortable silence stretched out, Bear got up. I watched her round form shuffle away slowly, padding toward the kitchen. I closed my eyes and listened to the familiar sounds of the shaken metallic rattle of old spoons and knives in a squeaky drawer, the unassuming shank when some toast pushed up, the soft pop of the refrigerator door as it opened, and then closed. When Bear returned, she surrendered to gravity as she fell into her chair, and pushed the little plate with her peanut butter toast next to her glasses on the table. She took a bite and crunched thoughtfully.

"You speak for all of us," she said.

I was silent.

"All your brothers and sisters – we were all pretty fucked up back then; good folks, but fucked up. Too tender hearted. That's why we were fucked up and on the street."

"I want to do a good job for everyone." My words sounded corny, inadequate. But I knew she wouldn't judge my words, but take my meaning.

"You'll do fine," She assured me over a mouthful of peanut butter and bread. "You're strong. You know who you are. It won't matter where they send you, or what they tell you to do."

"Thanks."

Bear nodded. I chewed on my recent memories, absently stroking my chin with my fingers.

"They asked me to cut my hair." I remembered suddenly and knew the telling would get a reaction.

Bear laughed, and then glanced at my dreadlocks. "You mean they don't want you travelling all over the country looking like some kinda freak?"

"Something like that," I admitted. I laughed, too. "They told me it would alienate people. They said I could forget about the *Today Show*. The producers told my agent that 'it was their responsibility to keep the public safe from seeing things that might make them uncomfortable.'"

Bear paused in mid-bite, looking at me incredulously. We both knew that statement was absurd on too many levels to start picking it apart.

"So what are you going to do, given that your hair is a public threat?"

"I'm keeping it, of course." I tried to be positive, to dredge up some faith in people.

"People will listen to me. I'm kind. I'm smart enough. They'll listen." I said it without conviction, but Bear nodded. Then she spoke with her mouth full.

"Be sure to show your tattoos, then, too."

In silence we passed the hours like we always did. I was glad for it. The people in New York had been kind to me, loving, really. I knew they thought I was a special person, someone who had triumphed over unspeakable adversity. They saw me as a rare example of the human spirit. To Bear I was just sonny. Bear knew that her life story, like mine, was a retelling of things that had all happened before. My story happened to a hundred people I knew, some who were still alive, and for whom living was a triumph. My story wasn't new. It wasn't a rare example.

After nightfall Bear and I went to Elliott Bay Books, the first stop on the promotional tour of my book. After she went to find a seat I lingered in the back of the room, waiting to be called to the front. Suddenly, a tall man moved to my side and stood, trying to make himself smaller while paradoxically trying to get my attention. When I looked at him, he smiled. He seemed nice. He was dressed warmly, even though it was the late spring, with a scarf protecting his smooth face.

"I read your book." He said to me softly, his gaze vague, directed perhaps toward a distant west.

"I'm glad." I said. "What did you think?"

After saying nothing for a moment, he finally turned to look at me, with the pained smile of someone who's endured a traumatic injury.

"Well," he said, "I liked it very much. But I worry that you have a dim view of the male sex. Don't get me wrong – I don't blame you. I just feel bad that you were, you know, a dancer downtown here, and all that. Maybe you don't like men very much."

There was something motherly in his speech. He was concerned for me. I suddenly pictured him making chicken and dumplings, making love, making lather in an old-fashioned shaving mug. I put my hand on his arm and squeezed it gently, because he didn't so much seem like a stranger.

"Some of my best friends are men." I chuckled. It made him smile. "There are many men I like very much, men I love. My father, my brother... Of course, not all men are the same." I paused. "I'm not even sure I know what makes a man a man, or a woman a woman. I think most of the time we just…pass."

He laughed again.

"Maybe." He said affably.

"Thanks for talking to me." I tried to make sure the warmth I felt was in my voice. "It makes me feel good that you were worried about me."

"I just felt like I had to say something to you."

I squeezed his arm again, and he turned to find a seat in the very back.

On the little stage, I perched on a small stool. I didn't want a podium, which would put something too solid between me and the people I was talking to. I always felt like podiums were for people who had something to hide, or maybe they were worried that their presentation would be so bad they would need a place to duck under while the audience threw rotten vegetables at them.

Bear sat in the front row with friends of ours who hadn't seen me in fifteen years, including Woody, whose wonderful face I'd always loved, with those eyes that seemed to look in every direction at once. I always knew she saw things other people didn't. There sat my friend Janet Planet, whose wild little daughter, Tomi Louise, was fathered by a drag queen, and other familiar faces. Somehow it broke my heart that they were all so proud of me.

At the end of my reading I asked Bear to come up to read a poem from the book. I introduced her as my dad. She read the poem with such a softness about her. At first those in attendance looked at her the way I had feared the people on the upcoming tour would look at me -- as if she were something on display, something to be figured out -- the Bearded Lady, a single act. But I saw their faces change as people listened.

As Bear stood there in front of everyone, comfortable in her skin, as comfortable as she had been looking in the mirror, suddenly she seemed at once brave and horribly vulnerable in her tee shirt, behind her blue eyes, tiny dustings of her silver whiskers still visible. She inspired the protectiveness you might feel toward a good woman, a feeling woman, and the admiration and faith one feels toward a good man, a feeling man. She was worth looking at.

This was it, I thought, the thing that summed it up for me: You are a freak until somebody loves you. I loved Bear, and nothing was wrong. Many loved her, and nothing was wrong.

Even if people didn't even know your exact gender, this first-pronounced trait didn't matter if you were loved; we all had nothing between our legs, nothing in our bloodstreams, holes in our sides, nothing and everything on our faces.

I wondered if it had been this way for all the bearded ladies, the ones who became traveling displays during the Renaissance, who became staples in the sideshow in its Victorian heyday. I think they had pride. I read that these women wore the best dresses, and were placed in elegant surroundings in which they struck feminine poses, their hair done in the latest styles. They were shown seated in front of mirrors, in front of husbands, people who loved them.

Why do we pass as men and women? Why do we pass as only half of what we are? The bearded women know. Bear knows. We are afraid of what we might give birth to, having made ourselves heavy with child.

At the bookstore, Bear finished the poem, her warm hand shaking a little as she still held the book in front of her. Then she lifted her face to the crowd. She smiled.

The Hidden Heart of the Mule-Faced Woman and the Science of Separation

It is hereby prohibited for any person who is diseased, maimed, mutilated, or deformed in any way so as to be an unsightly or disgusting object, to expose himself to public view.

City of Chicago ordinance, circa 1911

"One town... it was like the best town because everyone was like, I became an idol. I couldn't even go around town without people stopping me, like a celebrity."

Tallon Crawford, "The Bat Boy," 2004

I checked into the hotel in Chicago, my senses over-stimulated from the long plane ride from the west coast, the pointed, snaking din, and the hubbub of the airport. My way of coping was to shut down, draw in tight, and let my world become a small and manageable box. I could barely take in the ostentatious trappings of the hotel, though I knew it is one of the best. What made me sad, though, is that I couldn't see the man checking me in. I have something called face-blindness; out of context, under stress, I can't tell people apart, even good friends.

The faces of human beings are the first things to disappear when I feel this kind of anxiety. As the man at the hotel desk looked down at the computer screen, I moved the telescope of my vision to his eye, to the corner of his nostril, to his lower lip. I tried, but I couldn't put him together. I knew that if I saw him tomorrow I wouldn't know who he was. It doesn't matter how handsome or ugly he may be, he wouldn't ever exist as an image in my mind.

I found my room, almost at the top of the tall building. Outside the door was a brass plaque: *Author's Suite.* I wondered if I was supposed to feel important, or if there was something special about this suite that separates it in tone and feature from all the other rooms; perhaps it's bigger, perhaps more beautiful. What was beyond the door wouldn't really matter. I knew it was just another set of rooms, somewhere for my body to be, to eat, to sleep.

I turned the key and went in, wandering from room to room without turning on the lights, taking in the velvet expanse, the lights of the city far below through windows, the softness of it all, the lack of care the room had absorbed. No one had ever burned biscuits in here, or kicked the door, sick of poverty, or sat quietly in the corner, sewing a patch on, sighing for a better tomorrow. But I was sure that a string of authors had sat in its chairs, looking down at a world they hoped might be theirs; they had snored in the bed, shit in the toilet, had bad dreams, and looked worn in the morning, feeling like imposters.

The couch on which I sat received and caressed me. *Don't think about it,* it said; *Sit here and forget.* I sighed and reached in my pocket for an envelope a kind-looking woman had slipped into my hand just before I walked out of my last talk. I always found such notes touching. Most thanked me for writing, for affecting someone's life as intimately as if I had touched his or her body.

I opened the envelope. The card inside was beige and blue, my favorite colors, and I spent a long time looking at it from the outside, feeling this was good enough. But the inside was even better:

I held a copy of your book in my hands – the cover, your gentle, yet intense profile…. I thought you were beautiful. I began to read your book and felt an immediate understanding flowing, a feeling that perhaps it was possible that someone could comprehend life and me…. I get a measure of that daily as I read the Bible and communicate with the living God.

A small wave of happiness washed over me, as it always does when I know, for a single instant in time, that my words have gone out over that long, silent bridge and touched someone's life. It feels like an immense and mysterious accident to me -- as if I have saved someone's life by blinking at just the right moment.

What is odd to me is that she thinks me beautiful. Even as a child I knew I was ugly in a physical sense: not the way little girls usually think they are ugly, looking in the mirror over and over to make sure nothing unbeautiful has befallen them in a moment of inattention, but in a real, pragmatic way.

I always knew I was smart. I knew I had a lot to offer -- that, as my mother said, I might have a mission. I knew that I was good with animals and that I was a good artist; that I was good with words. I knew that I had a strong body, with unusual endurance and power. I knew I had good legs and hands. And I knew I was ugly. After carefully studying what was pretty in the culture I lived in, I simply knew, the way you know it's raining. It never made me sad. There were too many other things to think about.

Nancy Etcoff, a Harvard researcher, says that we live in an age of ugly beauty -- that beauty is now equal parts flesh and imagination, and that we imbue it with our dreams and saturate it with our longings. What I long for is to see everyone happy.

On the table next to me was a Chicago magazine called *Where*. In its pages I found fifteen female models, but only one was smiling. Four looked angry, and the rest looked lost, sad, or unapproachable.

I searched for evidence of happiness, or any kind of simple pleasure, as I turned the pages. There was none. In thirty-one restaurant ads, only two people were shown actually eating – actually enjoying the beautiful feeling of being nurtured by good food. In another ad Mona Lisa wore bright red lipstick. I thought about how the model for the original painting would feel, seeing her enigmatic lips flushed brilliant crimson. I wonder how the Italian master would feel about it, and I thought of the portrait of a feminine Christ, Christ the Bearded Lady, a beautiful, womanly Christ. Maybe beauty is somehow deeply connected to suffering.

Certainly we careen through life suffering, white-knuckled, looking for beauty…or its pale imitation. With this idea lingering in my mind I noticed that the bodies in the magazine I held were almost always snow-colored, their skin the hue of puffy clouds, or nearly transparent.

To attain this dead-white glow women in India, the Philippines, Africa, use what little money they have to buy products like Dr. Fred Palmer Skin Whiteners, Crusader Skin Toning Crème, Fade Out, and Venus the Milo. The bleach in these products burns the skin, leaves white spots on the body, and discolors fingernails with lumpy black and ochreous spots. It is painful, but the women continue to use it, day after day.

As I drifted off for a nap, I thought about sad, brown women, happy after they had died and lost all their color. Pale dreams. Ugly white nightmares.

I awoke later to find it was time to leave the hotel. Still foggy, I made my way downstairs. In the car to the venue I opened my eyes to look at the passing city. The Sears Tower rolls by high above, the Gold Coast, the other tall buildings seem so permanent. Yet after a fire started in a cow barn on Chicago's West Side on October 8th, 1871, much of the city was destroyed. I imagined the smell of charred beef, the smell of humans that roasted with them, burnt offerings on some primal altar of flame. The beautiful city gone in a flash.

They had mules pulling firefighting equipment then. They say that mules are stronger than either of their parents – a product of crossing a horse with a donkey. Unable to have children of their own, they give their bodies to the future in a different way. They have carried knights in tarnished armor, and taken us over mountains; they have traveled from darkness to light, bringing the heart of the earth out of our mines, making our own progress on their backs.

A score of years after the fire, a rebuilt and even more alluring Chicago would rise and prepare itself to fight for the right to host the Columbian Exposition. Many cities vied for the opportunity, including New York, Washington, DC, and St. Louis, but Chicago came out on top. Long and vociferous arguments on behalf of Chicago led it to be christened "the Windy City" by the New York Sun's Charles Dana – for its lung capacity, not its weather.

Opening in Chicago on May 1st, 1893, the exposition commemorated the 400th anniversary of Columbus' discovery of America with an aptly designated "White City" of fountains, where once there had been nothing but swamp. The exposition ran for six months and attracted nearly half the population of the United States at the time.

The official amusement area was known as the *Midway Plaisance*. Showmen sat on tall stools barking at the passing crowd, drawing people in under the cyclic shadow of the world's first Ferris wheel, capable of spinning 2,000 people at a time. Amid trained pigs and lions that rode on horses' backs, beside ostrich farms and hot air balloon rides, were villages where so-called "foreigners" could be seen in their "native habitats," in their "native clothes," eating their "native foods." Next to Irish, German, and Viennese villages were Dahoman mud-daubed huts carved with animals and birds. Each day the warriors, in grass skirts and armed with spears, treated the spectators to "war dances." Up the way fair-goers could ogle "cannibalistic Samoans in all their primitiveness." And there was an international beauty show: *40 Ladies from 40 Nations*.

In midway exhibitions like those of the White City, one could see what was being hawked all over the country as the highest, most permanent form of loveliness: the Circassian Beauty, with fantastically bushy hair, dressed in sumptuous silks of bright colors, pearls and capes. Presented as having exotic, dangerous lives full of suffering and insult, Circassian Beauties came from the Caucasus region of Europe, and were hawked as being swooning victims; they were at the mercy of cruel Russians on one side and tyrannical Turks on the other (doubtless trying to deprive the heroines of their virtue at every turn). The Circassian Beauty the crowd saw at the Columbian Exposition had been rescued from an evil Sultan who had bought her as a sex slave – and not a moment too soon.

The Caucasus region had a special significance to Americans, who were newly interested in anthropology and the pseudo-science of race classification. Johann Friedrich Blumenbach, a German anatomist, had introduced the term "Caucasian" when he argued that Caucasus was not only the origin of Europeans, which were the true Caucasian type, but of all humankind. The theory, then, was that the purest, most beautiful whites were Circassians, and that other people grew more degenerate as they migrated throughout the world. The farther away from the Caucasus a group of people were, the uglier they became.

Racial purity sealed the Circassian woman's beauty. She was the purest specimen of womanhood to be found on the planet. She was humble, modest, and intelligent – not to mention white as milk. This theme resonated in the minds of Americans, who were grappling with their own history of slavery. The Circassian Beauty seemed to suggest that no one, no matter how white, no matter how beautiful, was safe from the possibility of servitude, of misery, of powerlessness. But we could all be saved at the last minute.

Of course, the reality was different from what people saw. Then, as now, the women were props. In the public's eye and through the photographer's lens, they became what we *needed* to see. The real lives of the women were forgotten. In 1864, a hundred years before I was born ugly, one proprietor told a scout in Cyprus, to buy some women.

"I still have faith in a beautiful Circassian girl if you can get one very beautiful. But if they ask $4,000.00 each, probably one would be better than two, for $8,000.00 in gold is worth about $14,000.00 in U.S. currency… You can also buy a beautiful Circassian woman for $200, do so if you think it best; or if you can hire one or two at reasonable prices; do so if you think they are pretty and will pass for Circassian slaves.

Although the scout's trip was unsuccessful, a few weeks later a young woman showed up looking for work. There was nothing remarkable about her except that she had bushy hair. A week later, after a local Turkish resident was consulted as to the proper manner of dress and a suitable name, the young woman appeared before the public as a full-fledged Circassian. "Zalumma Agra, Star of the East," one of the most famous Circassian Beauties of all time, was born. This woman became the template Circassian and, in fact, the first example we have of a man-made freak.

The women who came after, almost all native-born Americans, wore little clothing rather than more, exaggerating not just their sensual appeal, but also their vulnerability. Many showmen claimed that their Circassian Beauty was the original one brought over by the scout John Greenwood. They continued to make this claim years later, which would have put their beauties at impossible ages, but the persistence of myth won out. Representation was everything, even though, as legendary circus press agent Dexter Fellows tells us, "The Circassian Sultana, Favorite of the Harem, was really an Irish immigrant from New Jersey."

In search of our own myths, like promises hidden under our stubborn skins, we carve out beauty, too. I studied the pictures of the Circassian Beauties and thought about the surgeries we submit to in this country. A result of healing the physical mutilations of World War II, plastic surgery brought reconstruction to soldiers who had fought against the fervor for racial and physical purity, against a regime that wanted everyone to look the same, that forbade by law the exhibition of freaks. We tried to reconstruct the wounded faces of soldiers who fought against an enemy who fanatically asserted that they could recognize anywhere the Jews they had sworn to annihilate. We fought against the evil idea that someone's appearance mattered.

Ironically, the first elective aesthetic surgeries were performed on Jewish people who wanted to eradicate their ethnic characteristics. Now a twenty billion dollar a year industry, aesthetic surgery gives us facial alterations, breast enlargements and reductions, liposuction on thighs, buttocks, arms, necks, and stomachs. We can reduce the size of our genital lips and enlarge our penises.

There is even a new diagnosis, BDD, or Body Dismorphic Disorder, applied to people who are addicted to plastic surgery. It afflicts about five million Americans. A woman in New York who took steps to sue her cosmetic surgeon for malpractice because, after twenty-nine years of plastic surgery procedures, she said he should have known she had BDD.

I saw a woman on television who had had twenty-six surgeries, including a brow lift at 25 years old, cheek implants, three nose jobs, three lip implants, and five breast surgeries. She rides a motorcycle without a helmet.

"I feel like if that's the way I'm meant to go, then that's the way I'll go," she said. I imagine her flying into the wind, flying into the ground, all her beauty so painfully gained even more painfully lost.

Professionals interested in the motivations for cosmetic surgery say that people obsessed with surgery are collectively expressing conformity to an ideal body image. I believe it has more to do with our drive to suffer for beauty, to sacrifice something, to undergo ordeals that somehow annihilate us, bring us close to death -- drained figures on shrouds of hospital sheets, rising again. Showing off our wounds to the surrounding faithful, we strive for union.

I think that striving is also why we starve for beauty. There were nuns in the middle ages who separated themselves from the world and fasted for days, for years, until with their deaths, their final sufferings and separations, they became one with everyone. Of the 261 holy women that lived in Italy between the 12th and 17th centuries, an estimated 80 systematically starved themselves over many years, until it killed them.

Like many young women starving themselves today, the saints started as girls devoted to the idea of perfection, felt a deep need for approval, were generous of spirit, and felt a relentless pull toward something higher. Appetite, pain, exhaustion, and sexual desire: All of these drives are grappled with, forced at last to be submerged or eradicated, bringing peace and the serene countenance of beauty.

Catherine of Siena started life in the 1350s. She was a happy, if homely child who loved to spend time outside, communing with nature. At five she began the ritual of saying a Hail Mary after each step as she climbed the stairs to her bedroom, eventually adding to her daily devotions elements of physical pain, like crawling and climbing on bruised and broken knees while praying fervently. After years of such rituals, Catherine began to refuse milk, meat, fruits, and breads. She stood through the night with her arms outstretched in penitential prayer. She stopped eating anything but the host. If she was forced to eat, she vomited.

Catherine found pleasure in treasuring pain. After becoming a nun, the Bride of Christ, she continued her self-denial. In ecstatic visions she spoke with Mary and the Host of Heaven. She was beholden to nothing but the power of God. Possessed of grace, she remained humble. After finally giving up water, Catherine struggled for a month, lingered, and then died. Though rarely herself towards the end, she remained immersed in the mystical union of all things she had sought throughout her life. She was beautiful.

Modern professionals tell us that a person with anorexia feels an underlying need to gain a sense of selfhood, of differentiation, to torture him or herself to discover their essence. What I believe is that Catherine, and all the self-starving people today, was suffering for the beauty of a union with all things. By seeing anorexia as a modern disease bereft of spiritual attainment we ignore the spiritual longing at its core.

Yes, these young women are starving to be beautiful, but not in the ways we believe. Out of our depth, we worriedly send them to treatment, always suspecting that they are selfish in their disease. The saints, though, were considered by the people who loved them as heroes, protectors. Their followers made pilgrimages to their tombs, sat in rapt attention as men preached the history of their holy deeds, fought for pieces of their bodies, certain that these fingers, toes, even a gaze upon the saint's lips, would bring them grace. My heart tells me it was given.

Back in my hotel room at the end of the day, I instinctively reached for my folio of freak photos and let the pages of the book in my hands flutter through my fingers until I find her. The Ugliest Woman in the World stares out from my picture book. Her name, which I thought fitting, was Grace, Grace McDaniels. Also called the Mule Faced Woman, she appeared at a sideshow at the Riverview Amusement Park in Chicago in the late 1950s. I caress her face with my gaze. Her nose, lips, and chin consisted of masses of lumpy tissue, and her face was covered with a port wine-colored birthmark, splashed like a lost sacrament across her features. Her mouth was deformed, her teeth jagged and sharp. Her lips, enlarged and distended, swollen and hanging down, made it difficult for her to talk. In the picture, she is trying to smile.

Grace got into show business when she won an ugly woman contest and began appearing as a freak. The first time she heard a carnival barker calling her the Ugliest Woman in the World, she complained to the Side Show manager. He said to her, "Look here, those girls in the girly show are beautiful and their bodies go in and out in the right places, and what do they get? $25.00 a week. And what do you get? $175.00 a week." The Mule Faced Woman thought about it and made no more complaints.

When Grace appeared for her portion of the show it was her habit to stand to the side of the stage with a veil on her head, waiting quietly like a contemplative nun, private under her prayer shawl. The barker would warm up the crowd, like a revivalist preacher, saying,

"In a minute I'm going to ask Grace to take her veil off so you can see for yourself what she looks like. You won't want to look for long. Instead, you will want to think of yourself, think how lucky you are that you aren't like her. Whether you are handsome or homely, beautiful or plain, you can thank your lucky stars that you are not Grace McDaniels, 'the Mule Faced Woman.'"

When Grace lifted the veil, the crowd would gasp; men and women alike would faint. Maybe they thought of what the barker said about lucky stars and believed Grace was cursed.

From Plato onward, many people have believed that physical beauty is evidence of spiritual beauty. *What is beautiful is good*, the Greeks said, and some part of us seems to agree. The idea was resurrected during the Italian renaissance. Philosopher Marsilio Ficino saw beauty as "the blossom so to speak of goodness." In 1586 Italian naturalist Giovanni Della Porta wrote *De humana physiognoma*, in which he sought to know the relationship between body and soul. Because he apparently found emotions and personalities unenlightening, Giovanni decided to compare humans to animals; the animal a human most resembled would determine that person's soulful qualities. If you look like an ass you are foolish, a mule you are stubborn, a rabbit you are timid, and if you look like a pig, you are greedy.

People who knew Grace, The Mule Faced woman, described her as a motherly, homespun person who was generous to a fault. After talking to her for five minutes, they said, you forgot all about Grace's deformity and saw…Grace. You became aware of her courageous heart. Many people loved Grace; she had more proposals of marriage than people could count. When she finally chose her husband, they had a long and happy marriage.

One woman, who had seen Grace during her engagement in Chicago some forty-five years ago, was horrified when she saw her face. But years later she learned that Grace was a wonderful person, that men were crazy about her, that "Amazing Grace" as the woman called her, "…had done better than other women who were 'just another pretty face.'' She went on: "We are told that God will someday make all things new and beautiful. I hope that when that great day comes we are given name tags … the first thing I am going to do is look through the crowd until I find Grace McDaniels. Then I will say, 'How do you do? It's been an honor to meet you.'"

Now I looked once again at the card I'd been given by my admirer: *She thinks I'm beautiful*. I tucked the card into my book and let it fall closed. I held the book against my chest. I am who I am -- whatever suffering has made me.

Maybe suffering *can* generate beauty. Albrecht Durer wrote that there lives on earth no person who could not be more beautiful. We suffer for who we are, and for who we are not. Suffering is all that is left. Beauty hurts us, and so we become one, the ugly and the beautiful, bound…bound. The word resonates in my mind.

Centuries ago Chinese girls bound their feet with tight bandages so that as they grew the bones of their feet folded in on one another. Tiny feet folded delicately in half. *A lotus in every step*. That is how admirers of the tiny, folded foot described it.

Our longing for beauty arouses our deepest fears; we respond to it viscerally, full of premonitions of death as we gingerly step toward it, our tiny hands and feet folded together in blossoming prayer, picking our way fearfully through beauty's field of mines. Killer legs, we say;

bombshell, knock-out, drop dead gorgeous, stunning, ravishing. We want beauty to enter us, to punish us, to burn us clean, to expose our pain and our terror, to excoriate and scar us, to make us beautiful in turn. This is the long trail of beauty's painful kiss, which cuts through time and distance. So we starve ourselves, cut ourselves, make holes in what covers us, letting inside out and the outside in.

Some holes I have read about bring into my thoughts the idea of opening a gate where beauty can either enter or shine through. Children have always been pierced by the Native American Tlingit, their parents throwing parties so all the children could be pierced at once. In ancient China and in Borneo today women wear heavy earrings to stretch their lobes. Lip plugs called *labrets*, are pushed through the lips of young people being initiated, as a decoration, a symbol of their trial. Gladiators pierced their genitals and tied them back between their legs. Whether or not this was done for practicality didn't matter – Roman women all wanted to be ravished by them, to bear their children.

In other painful extremes, the Suri women of Ethiopia stretch their lips with bigger and bigger clay or wood plates. Polynesian, South American, and Native American women and men have tattooed their faces in long, grueling sessions over long periods of time, the private skin a public canvas.

According to legend, Cleopatra had an inverted nipple and for beauty's sake had it pierced and stuffed with tiny pebbles to bring it back to aesthetic normality.

Many cultures incorporate scarification into their reflections of beauty. The process is extremely painful. Hook the skin, pull, slice, rub ash or dirt into the wound and repeat, over and over again -- the stinging kiss of loveliness. The result is a pattern of hundreds of raised scars, beautiful even in the dark. Such is the practice of the Karo of Ethiopia;

the Dinka, the Nuer, the Atuot, and the Bumi all have their own distinctive patterns that mark their tribe as the most beautiful.

American anthropologist Paul Bohannan witnessed the many beauty rituals of the Tiv of northern Nigeria, which included oiling and coloring the skin, chipping and filing teeth, and using Cam wood ash as a cosmetic. When he saw their rituals of total body scarification, which often take 25 years to complete, he was astonished.

"I once asked a group of Tiv with whom I was discussing scarification whether it was not exceedingly painful. They turned on me as if I had missed the entire point – as, indeed, I had. 'Of course,' one of them said, 'Of course it is painful. What girl would look at a man if his scars had not cost him pain?'"

Painful beauty. There seems to be so much of it.

While I was in Chicago, I decided to find someone to ask about beauty and its pain. After calling several modeling agencies, I finally arranged to meet Romana, a fashion and lingerie model, for lunch at a trendy restaurant close to Lincoln Park. She had been through fire, which she has openly described in a letter she sent to me before our meeting:

I feel that beauty is not about perfection, or a beautiful face, but about uniqueness. Everyone is beautiful to me or has beauty. Often times I have wanted to be a talent scout, or photographer, seeing the beauty in so many different looks. I am often told that I am beautiful and can "have whatever I want" because of it. It shocks me to hear this since I feel I don't have nearly anything I strive for. I still feel jealous or envious of others. Others make it sound as if I should be behaving in a certain way because of my so-called beauty. I am not heard when discussing with the girls the sorts of problems I encounter. I can relate to the loneliness. I believe that emotions are molded at birth, just as physical beauty is genetic. Now in my late 30's I am struggling to compete with younger girls and to maintain my own beauty. Maybe this is a sign of low self-esteem. Lots of times I feel that from the outside others think I have it all, but inside I feel like Marilyn Monroe, close to the end of her life, trying to make something happen. Maybe God gave me beauty because he knew I was weak on the inside and needed some sort of balance. I just don't know.

Now at the restaurant, I waited for Romana outside, though it was windy and cool. People were complaining that the wind was blowing things off their tables. From across the street, Romana approaches. The wind is blowing through her long, dark hair, her eyes are striking when the wind reveals them. Her jaw is set with strength, if not confidence. Although I can only see small snapshots of her face and form, it is clear that she is very beautiful by our society's standards. I notice I am not the only person watching her cross the street. Men and women both are spellbound as they keep their gaze steady upon her. She is professionally beautiful.

The waitress came and took our drink orders. I ordered a beer and when the waitress came back some time later she set it down too hard, spilling foam down the side. She then subjected Romana's water to the same treatment. She seemed unapologetic. I wondered for a moment whether Romana is often treated meanly by women, even the ones who are strangers, who are resentful of her looks. Romana seems not to notice.

I took a long drink of beer; it was colder than the wind. I thought of that funny tee shirt. *Beer: Making ugly people beautiful since 1846.*

Romana and I sat in the cold and talked about her family, clearly there have been only scarce pockets of warmth anywhere for her. Her father was mean and demanding. Romana was afraid of him. Her mother taught her about beauty in art, and in architecture. Mostly, Romana said, her mother sees beauty not in her, but in her grandchildren.

Romana was seven when she moved to Italy with her parents for a year and a half. *The age of reason,* I thought, *the place of the renaissance*. She told me about all the places she had gone, and the beautiful things she had seen. She enjoyed looking at things more than she likes being looked at. "People stare at me. But they never see me." She said with her eyes gazing far away.

"Yeah. I know. It's like that when you're ugly, too." We each nodded in agreement. Not that she agrees I'm ugly, but that she respects my own perception of myself, giving a gift that she is rarely given.

"It's like they don't realize that we can look back at them." She said.

"What do you see when you look back?" I asked her.

"It's too painful to look at for long." I was surprised to hear that she struggles with looking into people's eyes just as I do, and for the same reasons. I know it's because she really *sees* people.

Romana ordered a salad. She grazed on it while she talked about her depression and how she had to finally take medicine because she was in agony all the time. *Passerage,* I thought, watching her ruminate over her bowl of greens. *A French cress*. People used to use it cure madness, back when nature was part of our world.

Out of the blue, and clearly because she was proud, Romana told me that she was a patented inventor. I raised my eyebrows, not with surprise, but with delight – I could tell from the beginning that she was very smart. I hadn't seen this wonderful, childlike look of delight on her face during any other part of our talk, and I was anxious for her to go on. She explained in detail about the device she had invented, a complicated set of chambers that would prevent certain elements from passing through a set of barriers while letting other elements pass without any contamination. *Like the elements and barriers within all of us*, I thought, and I wondered if, on some subconscious level, her own life and spirit, her pain and near-forgotten joy had inspired her breakthrough.

As we relaxed more and more we talked about Romana's Italian, Catholic upbringing. She opened up about her faith. She believed faith is important; she believed in grace. She believed she wouldn't be punished for missing Mass, starving herself of the host. She said with a noncommittal sigh, "I have doubts and I have beliefs." As I watched her eat in silence I saw every woman who is sure that everyone else is happier, that every other woman is just a little prettier than she. For a moment she was the Mule Faced Woman to me, the ugliest woman in the world; then the wind gusted and she was every woman once more.

I thought about a passage I read a long time ago:

"An ugly woman rode into Arthur's court on a mule, announced a strange quest for the heroes of the Round Table. To be awarded the Sword of Strange Straps, one of the knights must rescue a maiden in a besieged castle of Montesclere. This sword would signify that this knight would be the greatest knight in the world…"

When we said goodbye Romana seemed more beautiful than before. I was sad that I have to leave her, a woman in an Italian castle with a sword and no knight, caught between heaven and earth, like the ugly woman and the mule.

When my escort picked me up again, we drove down Diversey Street. I laughed to myself that it sounded like "diversity" but it wassn't; and the people walking down the street all looked the same. It struck me that if I asked any one of the average masses of people walking down this street they wouldn't have thought that they were average. A poll taken not long ago revealed that approximately 90% of people believe they are "above average." The numbers would assert that that isn't statistically possible and that these people are not the beautiful thoroughbreds they believe themselves to be, but that they are really just mules.

I thought about mules again, putting out the burning flames in this city long ago. How out of place they would seem in the streets now, and how like the average mule most of us are. Although people might hasten to protest such a categorization, maybe it would help them to know that mules can do everything a million dollar horse can do: cut cattle, do roping and fancy dressage. A good mule can outdo a beautiful show jumper; a mule 50 inches tall can leap over a jump 72 inches high from a standing start. But wanting to be beautiful thoroughbreds, people jog and exercise, shop at the same clothing stores, move in and out of salons, becoming fit for the future by fitting in, just like everyone else. *Natural selection*, I guess.

I noticed as we drove that this was what would be called a "nice" neighborhood. In this neighborhood there weren't any people that would be thought of as "dangerous" or "suspicious." I thought of Charles Darwin's cousin, Charles Galton, who made layered composites of violent male faces – men convicted of mugging, manslaughter, and murder. The face he created would be a template of the degenerate man, ugly in behavior and evident by sight. The result surprised him, though: all the composite faces were attractive, their sins wiped clean as they became one.

In 1979, anthropologist Donald Symons considered this phenomenon and posited that we are attracted to the average, that beauty is the result of the cutting and pasting together of every face we have ever seen, a lifetime and world-wide average. Together we all become beautiful. The thought of being average suddenly struck me as a happy thing. I said it out loud, "I am average," forgetting my escort was there.

"Average!?" He laughed, "You're a celebrity! Get used to it!" In some sense he was right. I was packaged now. People treated me differently, listened to me more closely, thought my needs are important, thought I was beautiful without ever seeing me, or because they saw me differently. I wondered if Grace McDaniel ever felt like a real celebrity.

Later, as I spread out on the bed in my suite high above the ground, I thought of how far from everyone I am. There was an irony in the fact that when I had been without a home or a job, when I had nothing to eat, the comfort of people seemed so far away. Now that I was successful, closing my eyes in luxury, beauty brought happiness no closer, and people are still far away.

I thought about Romana somewhere in the city, lying in luxury, loveliness covering her pain. I thought of her being average, being beautiful. I hoped Romana's Christ, Grace, the Mule-Faced Woman's God, all Gods near and far, might take delight in the average beauty of our faces. I imagined a Buddha turning paler, looking out with bluer eyes. I imagined African masks in lonely museums shading charcoal to straw, changing from the blackness of fire to the color of lions. I imagined a darker Jesus, his brown eyes closed and his wide nose breathing in modern air, sitting on a mule that would take him home.

We pass as beautiful because the pain of longing itself makes us more beautiful. As I drifted off to sleep I felt the people of the city, of the world, one by one closing their eyes to the dark, to the light, to their riches, to their poverty, to the extremes of their circumstance, to their separation and fullness, to their suffering and ugliness, to their passing beauty being seen.

Passing Judgment

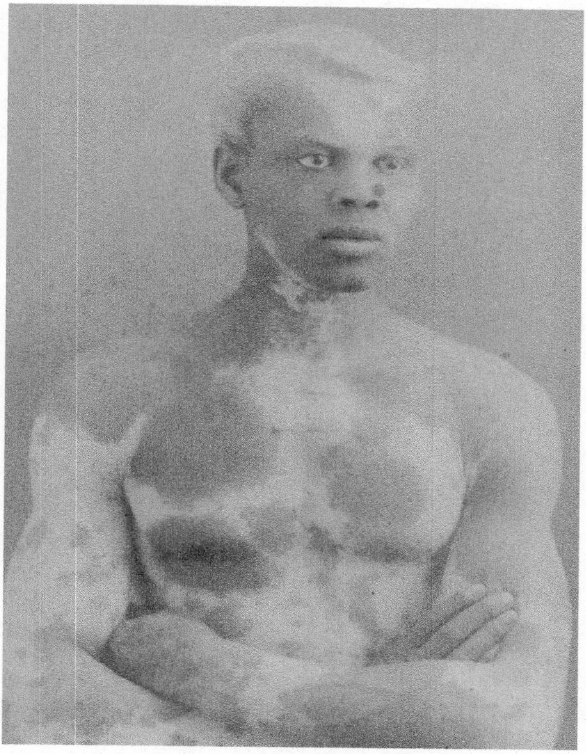

The Leopard Man and the Gorilla Judge

Before passing different laws for different people, I'd relinquish myself unto you as a slave.

From Franz Grillparzer's "Libussa" 1872

"Looks like a bunch of niggers to me."

So said a young white man who looked unblinking at the peaceful group of gorillas sitting quietly in their zoo shelter, beyond the viewing glass. The word "nigger" rang in my ears the way it dripped from his lips, heavy with emphasis. I had heard his declaration too often to be shocked, but not too often to be unmoved by it. I stayed silent. It seemed like there was nothing to say. He spat on the floor. In his fear he never took his eyes from the gorillas.

Fear was something I understood. Being born with my wonderful and terrible sensitivities, many of my days had been "a bright carnival of harm," as my writer friend Suzanne Paola puts it. Being what people now call autistic, I was afraid of the light that warmed the earth, afraid of the dark that cooled it, afraid of the human voices that filled the days between nights. Though I tried to understand what penance I owed when I was a child, nothing at that time explained why my softest clothes felt like sackcloth or why so much that I ate or drank was bitter. Swirling prizes from the bright carnival of harm were thrust at me like tiny, frowning clowns.

School made the carnival even brighter: the glare of false lights in the classrooms, the churning mob of children, moving, screaming. Clanging bells rattled the halls, announcing turns of the day where no one won any prizes; the bells seemed to mock the mark of time, over, over, and over again. Even though I loved to learn and my mind would travel far to escape what I felt as pain, I couldn't concentrate on anything my teachers said. I felt like I would explode as I tried to sit still and face forward to track a fraction of what was going on. I failed every test. I wouldn't listen when teachers and children asked me what was wrong with me. Everyone loves a carnival, after all.

By the time I was a teenager my circus was myself. The three rings full of busy thoughts that constantly ran in my head needed nothing beyond themselves. The tent between me and the world was complete. The animals of my imagination, the figments that helped me forget, filled my world and kept the harm away. The roaring of the lions and tigers in my head would make the sounds around me fade. The monkeys of my mind would run toward the sun, and all that was too bright and too colorful would be put at bay, eclipsed by the acrobatics of an inner life. The dark leopards of my inner sense of justice paced silently, endlessly, with nowhere to go.

People tried to breach the tall walls of my Big Top, to see the secrets that kept me so alone. Some knocked quietly or tried to lift the soft, canvas corners. Others tried to buy admission. Some tried to slash open the back wall with knives and attack the main attraction. Even though it was too late for me to share the show, I decided to take it on the road. The circus ran away from home and joined the world.

I couldn't take failing anymore, and I couldn't handle all the people wanting to get inside me. I was tired of the strain of a world assaulting my senses. I was tired of watching people who thought I was a freak kicking my normal places until they turned new colors. As winter neared, the time when most circuses fold up and go somewhere warm, I left home and went from cold town to cold town. Besides mastering my inner life I had no skills, so I couldn't find a job. I didn't know where there were people who would help me go forward, or who might help me stay if I wanted. I Remember sitting in a bathroom in a mall in a town many miles from home, looking at the dark rings under my eyes and the yellow ring of frostbite around my face. When the rings finally disappeared I went back outside. There was nowhere else to go.

I stayed homeless off and on for five years. Sometimes people let me stay with them, because they were kind or because they wanted to take something away. I think now that all of them were different kinds of circuses closing in the dark, just like me, stopping only to let their animals stretch, and void, and run in the courtyard. I traveled everywhere, going anywhere with almost anyone. Like most people who run away with the circus already in them, I did drugs to dull the pain of too much noise, too much light, feeling too much, seeing too much, hearing too much.

It was important to me, to my sense of what was right or wrong, that I didn't hurt anyone else, or steal what was theirs. But I broke the law in so many other ways – taking the drugs I thought would heal me, at least for a moment, engaging in victimless crimes: prostitution, public intoxication, vagrancy. Vagrancy: it's hard to believe that it is actually against the law to be homeless without any money, with nothing to eat, and nowhere to go -- but it is.

In Seattle, Washington, I took a job as a dancer in a tiny peep show arcade on First Avenue. I had been sleeping in a church stairwell on flattened cardboard boxes in the freezing cold. I used to go into dance clubs to stay warm and be near people, knowing I didn't have to talk to them. A woman saw me dancing once and told me I was good and should come down to dance where she worked. It was easy money, she said, and it was better than being homeless.

I danced on a closed-in stage with blood red carpet and mirrors all over the walls so that the customers, looking through tiny windows, could see all of me. They could also see themselves if they looked: husbands without wives, men with fantasies of dominating women, drunken men, shy men, lonely men, sometimes a woman. We all danced our pain away, making a silent deal with ourselves to never look for our own faces.

I felt like my soul was dying in this cold, industrial place. From the time I was a small child I found solace in nature. Nature was the only thing that seemed to nurture me. Now that I found myself in this city of endless mirrors, alienating in a way that unkindly went deep past the skin, I longed for the peace of plants and animals.

With some of the first money I earned as a dancer I went to the zoo in the northern part of the city, braving the bus, my hands shaking as I dropped my coins in the fare box. Nervously I watched the names of streets until I knew I was in the right place. I went to the gates and counted out my money again. I didn't like to look at people. It was hard to hold out my hand and reach through the little window to give money to the person selling tickets in the zoo's booth, meeting his gaze.

Finally finished with people, I went and drifted and stopped, meandered and paused, seeing the giraffes, the lions, the leopards, and the creatures in the nocturnal house. When I went around the corner and down the path to where the gorillas sat, my life was changed forever.

There amid the growing green and dusty red of the walls sat another kind of people that I felt I knew right away. They were big and solid and slow and silent. Somehow I knew they were aware of me as they sat there in the warmth of their dark skins. Somehow I knew that they wouldn't judge me for my crimes -- the ones I had perpetrated against myself or against the world; in the absence of human language there would be no sentences imposed.

For the rest of the day, I just sat near the gorillas, enjoying their stillness and solidity. When they looked at me, they did so quickly, and then looked away again. I would learn that this was a way of showing respect.

I came back to see them every time I could, sometimes every day. As the gorillas got to know me and expect me, I got to know them in turn. As I relaxed I could see why they did the things they did, and what they meant.

I began to see that underneath all the things we human beings say we are, we are only gorillas. As humans our needs are very simple in the end. We want to connect; we want to belong.

Over many years the gorillas gave me the peace and insight to start thriving in the human world. When I started treating human people as if they were gorillas I began to connect with them. Eventually I quit my dancing job and went back to school, working my way through community college and then university. Eventually I got a Ph.D. in Anthropology. It took many tens of seasons and many hundreds of hours sitting still near the gorillas, but through this long time the gorillas made me whole.

At this stop in the book tour I was in Denver. I was staying at the Brown Palace Hotel. The idea of a brown palace was fantastic to me and

I let my daydreams swirl like hot coffee with brown, creamy clouds, thinking how rich and sweet it would be if everything here was some shade of chocolate, as inviting as sable shade. I could be the shade of brown I had always dreamed of.

Alone in my hotel room I look down at my hands; as always, their paleness surprised me. It seems like I should have some outward sign of how much I had learned from observing the gorillas so intently, some obvious sign that I had been adopted by them, shared their skin. My teeth should be longer, or my hands should be black.

I had read about and envied a woman in one of my freak books, Hannah West; she was a white woman who lived in the early nineteenth century, 1811. She had a black shoulder, arm and hand. The rest of her was typically pale. A Dr. William Charles Wells had taken the time to turn her dark hand over and over in his own. Taking up his pen he described in neutral tones the parts of Hannah that were darker than any black person he had ever seen. He went on to speculate that Africans originally may have been white, but that evolutionary forces helped them adapt to the tropical sun.

People of the 1800s, especially abolitionists, were quick to seize on the idea that if white people could turn black, then maybe blacks could return to the white color of their original state. The idea of eradicating blackness offered hope to slaves. If blackness served as the marker of inferiority, when slaves became white, perhaps their masters would feel compelled to set them free.

There were many examples of the black body becoming white for them to cite. The fairs of the 1700s contained portraits, engravings, even souvenir coins, of black people becoming white, with black and white rendered in a rich palette of original art that encouraged throngs to come and see "The Leopard Child," "The Leopard Woman," or "The Leopard

Boy." Their arms, legs, and torsos were mottled maps of some mysterious place they had unexpectedly come from, glimpses of a white country in a black sea, or a black continent in a milky ocean.

Like streams of milk chocolate, the Leopard People found their way into these fairs, and into taverns, dime museums, and sideshows.

Even in academic settings the "spotted Negro" was put on display. At a meeting of the American Philosophical Society in 1786, Dr. John Morgan presented a "motley coloured, or pye Negro Girl and Mulatto Boy." Morgan distinguished between what he called the "dead white color" of the regular albino, already Caucasian, and the encroaching color on the bodies of the black children he exhibited to the society. He declared their growing depigmentation, a "beautiful lively white." Morgan divided the quick the dead, appealing to a society afraid of both death and blackness.

The Philosophical Society was again treated to a viewing of a spotted man when they invited Henry Moss to attend a meeting. In 1796 Moss had begun showing himself in taverns around Philadelphia. Even President George Washington went to see him. During the Revolutionary war Moss had served for six years as a soldier; after that, it is said his black color "began to wear off," and "his wool" began falling out, with straight hair growing in its place. White people believed that underneath the black man Henry Moss, was a white one pushing its way out. Blackness, they assumed then, concealed a common whiteness, a common humanity.

The people of the day looked for explanations. They invoked the Bible, especially Jeremiah 13:23: "Can the Ethiopian change his skin, or the leopard change his spots? Then may ye also do good, that are accustomed to do evil."

When a doctor, Benjamin Rush, viewed Henry Moss at the Black Horse Tavern, he had just seen the effects of yellow fever in Philadelphia, where the epidemic had killed one in every ten people. Dr. Rush believed that the arrival of ethnic immigrants was to blame for the virus. After viewing Henry Moss he came away convinced that his black pigment was the result of some kind of contagion, the "effect of a disease in the skin of the leprous kind." Rush concluded that "Negroes…should be pitied and maybe quarantined, for the pestilential threat they carry with them." He offered evidence of the danger of becoming black by telling the story of a white woman "who not only acquired a dark color, but several of the features of the Negro, by marrying and living with a black husband."

Regardless of what Rush had to say, Henry Moss took his money and the money of any others who came to peer -- to propagandize, or to appreciate – it made no difference to him. He used the earnings to buy his freedom.

Looking at my own pale hands, I wished that it could be so for me -- that the ways I'm a slave in this culture, in this body, could be paid off in the currency of pain, and left behind. I could see no sign in the mirror of my own transformation into beautiful blackness. There was only silver and white, and sometimes empty eyes that looked for a reflection. I looked at my white hands, holding my book of freak photos, all there in black and white, with no trace of white lies, or black hearts. Maybe in some ways we cannot change our spots. We must wear them.

I thought about the gorillas that saved my life -- my first tribe. Their round, black faces looked at me from my own past. I wished I could bring them with me. They would stare at all this opulence in wide-eyed wonder, and go away caring about not only whether the fruit was good, but more importantly, whether an understanding of things around them had been gained. They are almost always open like that. Because of their open and generous nature it hurt me when people called them ugly monkeys or hurled racial epithets at them.

I thought of the colors of people, of animals, the colors of our real selves – colors that can't be seen. And I thought of the ways people muddied those colors with hate or ignorance. I had a lump of reactive anger in my throat. It was red.

That evening I arranged to take a break from the bookstore readings and media interviews of my author tour. Instead of going out to talk, I was staying in to listen. I went downstairs to meet the Honorable Robert Patterson, "Beau" to his friends. I'd come upon his name almost by accident as I looked for information about leopard families; I was searching for stories about the history of black people and the law.

Beau grew up in the impoverished Five Points community in Denver, not far, but a world apart, from the hotel we were now meeting in. He was the baby boy of a janitor and a maid. In an age when there were more black men in prison than in college, Beau worked hard to succeed, even though he thought all of his brothers and sisters more talented than he was. Beau was the first of his family to graduate from high school, and after that first to graduate from college. Then he graduated from law school.

In 1985 Beau was appointed judge of the Denver County Court--the first African American in history to preside over the court. He directed a seventeen-member bench and served as the appointing authority for almost 300 employees of the court. Prior to his appointment, Beau had been the state's Assistant Attorney General. Earlier in his career he served as both Colorado and United States Public Defender. Amid all this, what impressed me most about Beau was that he had had a vision for the Denver County Court that focused on the user of the court system.

With benevolent leadership he had reworked the system so that its quality would exceed the expectations of people using it; he believed that customer satisfaction should drive the courts. By listening to the *people* he moved the court, as an institution of fair adjudication, toward providing an environment where dispute resolution and criminal proceedings took on a new immediacy, and offered a deeper kind of satisfaction. He wanted to lead people to justice. Beau's approach was based on collaboration and cooperation with the community; he allowed its members to partner with him in designing and delivering justice services.

Beau was like a silverback gorilla that grew up in a family and then at some point took it over, leading its members to the best resources. It is this gorilla who steps in to settle disagreements between those smaller than him, less powerful – it would be he who kept his community together and risked his life, his heart, for their safety. I was so impressed with all Beau had done that I wrote to him and told him so; it was the greatest compliment I could give. I wanted to know Beau. I asked him if we could have dinner when I was in Denver.

In the lobby of the hotel I saw Beau through the crowd. I would have known him anywhere, even if he had been trying to hide, which he would never do. He exuded a sense of great presence, of grounding and self-possession. I felt like I was seeing an old and beloved gorilla leader and put my hands out to him, feeling humble and small.

We talked about the lives of our days as we walked to the hotel restaurant. The staff clearly knew him and was happy to see him and led us to our table right away. It occurred to me that I had never seen such deference at a restaurant before. I wondered how the staff would have treated me if I was there alone – the way I looked, my obvious oddness, the inattention to proper clothing I can't seem to overcome; I wondered if in some kind of silent segregation they would have set me at some isolated table.

After we had ordered drinks and appetizers we started talking about his legal career. He shared many stories, some that were funny, some with predictable endings, some surprising.

Beau told me that one day a defendant standing before him expressed a concern that his case was being heard by a black judge. A predictable hush fell over the 150 people sitting in the courtroom as Beau fixed him with an objective stare and said firmly, "I will tailor a sentence that recognizes who you are and gives you the tools so you won't ever have to stand here as a defendant again." The man before him was black.

"It's unusual for judges to adjudicate in the places they grew up. People who knew me as Beau or 'Little Beau' now come into my court. Sometimes I recuse myself, because it would be hard to be objective." As I listened to Beau's words I thought about a black man I had seen on Jerry Springer's show, who wanted to join the Ku Klux Klan. *Yes*, I thought, *sometimes it is hard to be objective*.

"But it is important to the community that I'm there." Beau said, bringing me back to his own experiences. Everyone knows the story of Jesus and his sage words -- that a prophet is never appreciated in his own land. Of course people would see you forever as a peer: a brother, a sister, a grandson, even a baby. That Beau was able to overcome this was testament to his great power as a man. The special gorillas who lead are like that, too. It is an amazing feat.

And even more, Beau was able to overcome other prejudices than those of the people who grew up with. Challenges clearly excited Beau.

As we sat together in the restaurant, he talked excitedly about his deepest beliefs, as if we were old friends. I loved him right away for that; the fact that he has seen so much – both alone and in his front row seat as a judge – and yet was still unguarded, and saw positive potential in everything. If there is anything shadowed in Beau, anything dappled for camouflage, I couldn't see it. I asked him if there was anything about himself he has had to hide in order to succeed in his work.

"Yes, there is." He grew serious. "When I put on my robe, I have to cover myself—all my prejudices, predilections, and biases. My robe is the cover I put between myself and professional objectivity. The judicial robe is woven not only of the fabric of authority and power, but also of responsibility and humility and through it the administration of justice. It can hide you, but it also affords you the opportunity, the privilege, of expanding yourself. Sometimes when I take off the robe I get a liberating feeling. Ahhhh."

He smiled and stretched. I had a sense that he didn't ever simply shed his ability to be penetrating but fair, judicious and controlled, like some sleek hunter. He looked at me with a tenderness I couldn't translate, as if with his practiced and unobtrusive eye he saw me in some new way I could never see myself. He went on.

"The judge's robe is the mark that he who wears it has a sacred duty to perform. I won't walk out of the courtroom wearing that black robe." He paused and then suddenly burst into his infectious giggle.

"Can you imagine me running down the courthouse corridors with my robe flapping in the wind?" I did laugh at the thought. For a moment I saw him like the old people who could still see him as Little Beau. I imagined him as a child with a robe ten sizes too big running down the hall with the same giggle. I loved his laugh. Then, like a shadow passed over the sun, he was serious again.

“Sometimes I look over the mass of humanity sitting in my courtroom and think ‘What manner of dysfunction will I see today? Will I have to decide whether she shook that baby when it wouldn’t stop crying, or did the baby fall out of the crib? Will I have to decide whether the police officer was too rough on the rowdy, intoxicated person leaving the market, or if the person was really resisting arrest? Will I think of my grandchildren and recoil when I hear about the baby’s injuries? Will I think of my young son and how he and his buddies get loud when they occasionally get together after work to have fun? No… I have to cover myself.”

I thought about Beau’s long black robe. He was every man who ever had to be more than one color at a time, who lives in different worlds at all times. I thought of little holes or rustling partings in the black, where the colors of Beau’s best intentions show. He is human. He could never be completely covered in justice, but his robe helped him become closer to his conception of the ideal person. I thought of all of us who truly want to be better and better people and the mantles we assume, hoping we grow into them, knowing they are a little too big for us just at this one moment.

Because Beau is so good a human being, I simply couldn’t think of him as neutral in the complete sense of the word. Power was his job. I remembered that in many African tribes only royalty can wear leopard skins. Maybe that pattern captures the black of justice dappled liberally over the brown skin of humanity. Beau commanded this respect. Like a gorilla, like a leopard, he was absolute in his measured might and people knew it. There was no doubt.

A waiter smoothly interrupted us to give us a complimentary dish from the kitchen. Beau and I looked at it appreciatively and thank him. I searched the waiter’s face. The gift seemed genuine, a token from people who knew Beau was and truly respected him. People will do anything for a good leader, for the light and shadow of a king.

I tell him that is why I think they brought the little plate of food. Beau knows I'm right, but he remains humble, self-effacing. He says he thinks it is all in the title.

"My name is Robert, also Beau; I have a lot of names. But in my twenty years on the bench they have all been absorbed by 'Judge.' That title can open a lot of doors, do a lot of good. But inside it's almost as if I have a separate identity."

When I told him I believed that things were finally changing now, that people were more likely to look deeper and try to really know a person before they judged them, regardless of the label or title they had been given, he looked thoughtful.

"I grew up in what was called the ghetto. I didn't know that's what it was. I had a very happy life and I had all the things everyone else in the neighborhood had. I didn't grow up feeling oppressed. When I got to high school I realized things were significantly different. I had a high school counselor tell me I would probably be a fry cook or work on a train. I was furious -- furious and determined. I credit him with a lot of my success. His negativity kept me motivated whenever I met a challenge. Later, when I gave my fortieth high school reunion speech, I mentioned him. I also wondered out loud if he had any outstanding traffic tickets." We both laughed, because something about real justice is funny.

"Despite Mr. Gardener, I applied to University of Colorado. I got in and had to work to pay my tuition. I worked nights and went to school in the days. I remember one of the first classes I took was ethics. I remember sitting in that class wondering why I didn't know what the other students knew."

I was distracted by the thought that someone with the name Gardener could operate with such disregard for blossoming. Maybe he thought it was his job to prune the flowers of disappointment before they bloomed too large. Beau continued.

"There were concentration camps here around Denver. They called them 'internment camps' then, built for the Japanese during World War II. I went to school with a lot of their children when I attended University of Colorado. The student body was very diverse; we had inter-racial dating and everything. I thought the whole world was integrated…."

I sat looking across the table at his robed disappointment. It was hard for him to cover his feelings about these things. There is something so wearying about being noticed in a negative way for things about yourself you don't even think about, that have no physical or personal meaning for you.

Perhaps because I was still and quiet and learned to blend in seamlessly with my family on the other side of the glass at the zoo, it seemed that often the public didn't notice me; I was as mute as the glass they looked through, as distant as the gorillas they stared at. It was easy for me to see the world as integrated in those moments, but then the moment would be broken. I would hear the ugly words, the ones said, shouted, or hissed, even whispered. It made no difference: loud or hushed, the sentiments were the same.

Though it was less common to hear someone actually use the word "nigger," their beliefs and feelings about the gorillas could be summed up in the same word. The gorillas were the scary brutes that providence had dictated; they were big and lowly and black. They unsettled us; not like us, not related to us. Hence it is right that we enslave them. The people who perform these rituals of division do so with a cutting need to be included among those who aren't on the other side of the glass.

We cut gorillas apart from us, like any marginalized people, and the cutting is literal. People eat gorillas all the time. You can buy a good smoked one in the Congo for twenty American dollars. Eat them before you see their humanity, before you can look them in the eyes and see who they really are. Pay your money and slice a bit of chewy muscle off to fork it into your mouth, like a treasured guest at God's dining table.

A slave trader named A.J McElveen once remarked about a captive black man that he was in hurry to sell, " I think him very prime… his Equals cannot be found in capacity…he is a Genius, and it is Strange to Say I think he is Smarter than I am."

No doubt A. J. MacElveen would think of Beau Patterson as a freak, like the ones in my collection of photographs: a different kind of Leopard Boy. I imagined people lining up to see his power behind the curtains of centuries past. He would be like Henry Moss, standing naked and proud, covered in black with other colors showing here and there -- counting coins and criminals, waiting for freedom. It made me feel sad that in this way, nothing has changed. Like everyone before and now, Beau was a freak in chains. Just another animal trying its best.

I put down my knife and fork and fixed Beau with a stare. It occurs to me that he is the perfect person to ask, "What do you think separates humans from other animals?"

Beau thought carefully. Being wise, he started by telling me he had no empirical evidence to support his claims.

"I suppose intelligence…a need for group affirmation… an ability to love…. language… hmmmm… compassion…"

"Animals have all those things," I said, and he smiled, leaning back, ready to hear the argument. For a moment I thought of the times during the Inquisition when animals appeared in court and were allocated a defense counsel; their grunts and whines were interpreted as denials of guilt or confessions. Black dogs and monkeys were hanged for their crimes, like black people, lynched in a freakish carnival. The law of the jungle: We decide who is black with white spots, and who is white with black spots; we decide who is human and who is animal. This is the real history of the human circus: the law of who gets to be us.

I explained to Beau the ape intelligence studies my friends do, and the fact that one gorilla described the death of his mother in Africa through sign language, and how he was taken away as a baby. I told him about the ways gorillas are there for each other, how I have seen them express love and compassion. I told him about the ways that gorilla men see it as their highest duty to preside fairly and compassionately over their families.

We talked about why people believe animals, even the gorillas I knew, belong behind glass. We talked about the fact that these reasons were the same ones given in defense of black human slavery: they are inferior to us: they have no moral character, no self-control, and no ability to understand laws. If they were free to interact with us as equals, they would be a danger to themselves and others. We have a right to claim them as property. It's for their own good.

Writing ten years before the abolition of black slavery, Josiah Priest, the author of *A Bible Defense of Slavery*, examined the idea that "Negroes" may have originated from a white woman's fright at seeing the hideous monster, the "black ourang-outang" in the antediluvian wood. We are reminded by the Reverend Priest that St. Luke testified that black persons could not have possibly come from a shared progenitor of humanity (in this case Adam) for a reason he felt was obvious *prima facie*: Adam was a white man. Further, Priest said, it was obvious to anyone with sight that the physiology of black people, so familiar in our present descriptions of gorillas, could not allow any reasonable person to believe that "Negroes" were of equal humanity.

Josiah Priest gives us a list of specific physical attributes (the emphases his), in case we forget where to look: " …the *color, formation, woolly* hair, thick *skull*, pointed *posteriors*, *large* foot, pouting *lips*, wide and *flatted* [sic] nose, *low* forehead, hollow and compressed temples, *narrow* monkey shaped waist, *wide* chest, [and their] angular shaped legs." Blacks were not people by the Will of God and the natural order; they were numbered and faceless animals in their captivity, inventory in slaving ship log books, in the notes of slave traders, and even in the scientific papers of men in ivory towers.

Beau and I talked about the persistent need that most people in power seem to have for a "dividing line" or a set of characteristics that keeps different sets of people away from them.

I told him that one thing I learned at the very beginning of my training as an anthropologist was that early scientists in my field tried hard to infuse their assessments with scientific distance, and unflinching objectivity. They felt that the admission of human feelings would, in a logic that seems counterintuitive now, render them unfit to perform their work.

The original arbiters of humanity set about to find unshakable criteria for what made a person a person. They believed language was a good measure, and so it was that Linnaeus, the first person to classify all living things, set mutes aside as a different species. Johann Christian Hoffman, visiting Southern Africa in 1671, asserted that the San people were not people at all, but brutes, because they could only cluck incomprehensibly; he believed them to be "stupid beasts."

In fact all darker-skinned people were believed to be more closely related to apes than to the rest of humanity: their coloring, the "oblique forward angle of their teeth," their "general anatomical structure," all were taken as evidence that they were "inferior animals." Australian aboriginals, Tierra Del Fuegians, Fijians, Native Americans, Kamchatkans, and Chinese – all were believed to be subhuman. It was obvious to everyone (but them, of course) that they were not the same as the rest of humankind.

Even people we now think of as "white" were declared mistakes of nature. Moors and Basques, Mediterranean island people, the Irish, and Slavs all fell far short of qualifying as human beings at one time or another. Of course, now we know better. We can all agree on what is – or is not – a person. For example, everyone knows that apes are not people. It is insulting to compare a group of accepted humans to them, unless – and this is telling -- the ape happens to be white.

I told Beau about the time I came across some striking pictures of "Snowflake," a white gorilla who was captured as a baby in Central Africa and eventually bought and exhibited in the Barcelona zoo. On finding this picture I had seen an opportunity to probe the prejudice I saw in front of the gorilla exhibit each day. Realizing that the only difference between Snowflake and all the other gorillas I had known was that he was white and that they were black, I copied a photograph of his face and took it to the zoo. The picture I found was a close-up of his pink face as he fixed the camera with a probing gaze. His eyes, like chipped blue marbles, were bright.

I kept the picture in my satchel as I sat in my regular corner of the public viewing area of the gorilla exhibit. At random I would greet zoo visitors after they had watched the gorillas for a while; then I would whisk Snowflake's picture out of my case and show it to them. The comments I heard bore out my suspicion that racial perceptions were at the heart of our culture's attitude toward my black family.

Of Snowflake people said,

"He looks so *HUMAN*!"

"He could live in my neighborhood."

"Wow! I bet he is really smart! What is his IQ?"

"Can he do things that other gorillas can't do? I bet he could."

"He would make a good father."

"Those eyes really make you think. It's like a *person* staring back at you."

"God must have a special purpose for him."

One little girl visiting the zoo in her Sunday dress pointed to my friend Pete, who was sitting near us behind the glass. "That gorilla is mean." Then she pointed to the photograph in my hand. "That one is nice."

I showed Snowflake's picture to between fifty and seventy-five people over the course of several weeks; almost all their answers were variations on the quotes above. And the color of the human people who said these things—black, brown, or white-- didn't make a difference.

Many times I wished I'd had Snowflake's picture when the young white man called the gorillas "niggers." I would have given anything to see the dark look pass across his face as he tried to make light of it all. I've always had to laugh at the idea that man is the "rational animal." If this were true, we wouldn't fume about people with thirteen items getting in the nine-item express line at the grocery, or watch bad television, or nurse our prejudices.

Today when we consider people's prejudices about other kinds of humans, most of us feel repulsed. Comparing humans with other animals has gone out of fashion, but it was common during the early history of the circus and the sideshow. Black men in leopard skins and loincloths, clutching cowhide shields and spears, bizarre and wild, played the parts of savages, cannibals, and beasts. Billed "The Hottentot Venus," Saartjie Baartman, a member of the San tribe in the Kalahari, was exhibited in London from 1810 to 1811. She had the large buttocks of women of the San. Though it was the only feature, other than her color, that seemed unusual, calling her "Venus" was clearly intended as a joke. She was barely human to the crowds, let alone beautiful.

According to an article in the *London Times*, she was kept for exhibit in a raised cage, "like a wild beast…ordered to move backwards and forwards, and come out and go back into her cage… like a bear in chains." Once she tried to use a guitar she had been playing to hit a man who laughed at her -- but her "keeper" raised a bamboo cane in warning and she stopped, terrified. The trainer proclaimed her to be "as wild as a beast." He dressed her in a skin-colored garment to make her look naked, and invited interested spectators to touch her.

Prospecting showmen sent scouts to buy Africans and bring them back to put in shows as main attractions. In 1930, one entrepreneur brought thirteen women with lip plates and two men from the Congo to become showpieces in Europe for two years, after which John Ringling, of Ringling Brothers Circus, booked them for a U.S. tour. Side Show manager Clyde Ingalls retooled the exhibit, promoting it as "the World's most Astounding Aborigines – New to Civilization – Mouths and Lips as Big as Full-Grown Crocodiles --the Crocodile-Lipped Women of the Ubangi." It didn't matter that Ingalls made up the name "Ubangi," or that the women's lips weren't that big: the crowds filled the big tent.

“Clicko,” lite Saartje, was also a San, billed as an authentic African bushman. He would stand next to the carnival barker, dressed in leopard skins, and dance and yell in San at the top of his lungs. What was he shouting? Maybe, “I want to go home now.” Or, “You people are total suckers.” That’s what I imagine him yelling in the heat of the summer crowds under a white sun, shouting over the story of his capture The story went that he was caught by a Captain Du Barry, who, after killing several ostriches pursued Clicko, thinking at first that he was just another ostrich.

Another ostrich?! Regardless of the laughability of the story Captain Du Barry was lauded for having brought Darwin’s Missing Link, the evolutionary step between gorillas and men, into captivity.

Of course, Clicko was only one among many black missing links. Every show had one. The press and the proprietors called them such things as crosses between “a nigger and a baboon,” or “an advanced chimpanzee.” A long series of acts called “What Is It?” displayed African Americans draped in fur from head to toe, “Dog-Eating Missing Links from the Philippines,” or “Savage Indians.”

Showman George Middleton relates an awkward incident when two black women came to see the ferocious Zulu warrior shown at the O’Brien Circus in 1884. As the warrior sat there on stage with his ringed nose and animal hide robes, the two women came close and scrutinized him. “See this nigger?” exclaimed one, pointing indignantly. “He ain’t no Zulu. That’s Bill Jackson. He worked over here at Camden on the dock.”

As it turned out, many of the Zulus, the Wild Men from Borneo, the Dohomans and Cuban Wonders, were local people just trying to get by; it didn’t matter where they were really from, or who they really were. I wondered about the way it must have been for Bill Jackson, trying to keep his insides separate from his outsides, trying to put his shield between himself and the women who recognized him, and for all the others like him who were trying to go beyond what people thought they were or weren't, as they moved across the country in search of any kind of life at all.

Then, as now, there were no territories that remained free from the dusty portage of judgment. The crowds brought their territories with them. Beau understood this.

As our dinner wound on, Beau started to talk about different civil rights cases that covered these territories and his prodigious knowledge and seemingly photographic memory was staggering. In 1857, for example, a few years before the census, the Supreme Court ruled on the Dred Scott case and judged that blacks had no rights that whites were bound to respect, and further, that the government was powerless to decide the issue of slavery in the territories.

The first Governor of the Colorado Territory, William Gilpin, had not supported the vote for blacks, even though an African American had briefly held the post of Assistant District Attorney of Arapaho County. The man eventually left his post for the Montana gold fields. Some historians have noted that he "hated his race." I wonder if he tried to outrun it.

When blacks began making their way into Colorado as early as 1879, the white citizens became alarmed. Thousands of black emigrants, seeking the gold of a free life and a turning of the color of their fortunes, left Mississippi, Louisiana, Alabama and Georgia to seek opportunities in the north and west after their emancipation in the south.

At one point, a meeting was held in a courthouse in Denver to discuss the problem. A Judge Elliot came to give his remarks. He was in favor of black immigration, and believed in the spirit of independence and the power of the human will to uplift. He said, "It is…only when a people rises up in its might and works in union for the purpose of its own elevation that it succeeds."

Judge Elliot recalled that when he was in law school there were no blacks allowed on juries and the testimony of a black witness was without value because they had what was euphemistically called "council disabilities." He went on to thank God that now all men's testimony was valued in measure with the man's character, and that in his current position on the bench he saw black jurors called almost every day. He went on to assert that if he had to pass sentence on a man who didn't have the same civil rights he did, he didn't think he could do it. The heart of good judging, I say.

Interestingly, 139 years before I sat in Brown Palace and had dinner with Beau a very different Judge Patterson, the Honorable Thomas J. Patterson, gave his opinion to a gathering in the courtroom.

"As to whether a large influx of southern Negroes into Colorado will prove beneficial to the Negroes, or advantageous to our present population is a very serious question. But I venture to predict that if an influx of southern Negroes comes to Colorado, thousands of those who now denounce southern people on account of alleged persecution of the Negroes would become their persecutors in turn because their wages and the comforts of their families would be curtailed."

The black and white predictions of that earlier Judge Patterson were prophetic, as the mottled history of race and power took on a dark mantle in Colorado, and all over the country. As Beau and I finished dessert we both agreed that we thought we could believe that things were getting better for people. In the back of my mind I had the sad, passing thought that it wasn't getting much better for gorilla people, or other animals whose values have not been truly allowed to shine out from the shadow of prejudice. Maybe it would just take one person and one person and one person seeing their worth – that's how it has happened before.

After dinner, I walked Beau out to the lobby. I kissed him on the cheek and gave him a big hug. I was so happy to have met him and sad when he walked away. As I followed him with my gaze on his way through the door I imagined him in different times and places, being the same man, draped in the same regal robes, a symbol of times past. No matter when he lived he would have been a missing link, a dark animal in dark skins, seeking justice. He gave me hope.

In my hotel room in the morning I called room service for breakfast. A black man brought it to me. I thought of all the reasons he wouldn't look at me. It might be training, professional deference; it could be that like me and Beau, he is uncomfortable with eye contact. Maybe he was resentful of me for staying in a hotel he couldn't afford. *Brown Palace, indeed.* For a moment I fought the urge to tell him I didn't belong in such a place either, that I couldn't afford this hotel, that I belonged in the jungle, with the gorillas.

I fought another urge--to ask the man if he ever wished he was back in the jungle. I knew he would be deeply offended, that such a question would stab at an open wound. I knew he couldn't understand how well I understand those wounds, or how much I want us all to be able to show our true colors. Instead, I smiled an acquiescent smile and asked him if he wanted to stay and watch the black and white episode of the Twilight Zone that I was watching – the one in which the guy who wants to be left alone to read is delighted that he is the lone survivor of the a nuclear holocaust until he steps on his only pair of glasses, and then spent the rest of his life as blind as a bat.

I knew the man who brought my food would never stay with me, knowing that now he probably thought that I was crazy, someone with a "council disability," as Judge Elliott had described black people. Still, I longed to hear his secrets, hidden by a darkness that has nothing to do with skin or justice, and having more to do with the crimes of being human.

I ate my breakfast, alone now, but propped up just across the table from me was a picture of a Leopard Boy; a young black man with white spots here and there over his body.

Before my trip across the country I rarely thought about the ways that "normal" people were faced with the joys and cruelty of their difference. I was so consumed by the struggle to survive that I found it hard to see past the bars of my own cage. After that, I was fully immersed in the gorillas' world. When I considered other human beings I thought of them as having no weaknesses, like gods in the garden, beyond natural law. Now I was seeing that they were frail, prone to the worst kind of judgments from within and without, freaks of nature subject to the rulings and sentences of every other freak.

I thought about how the African-American man in the freak picture looked in ways like the gorillas I had come to love, but with patches of my own skin. To me, comparing any person to a gorilla not only doesn't diminish the human, but is in fact a rare and exalted compliment. In my own mind such a comparison could never diminish a human person.

Many weeks later, when I got home from my book tour, I saw Beau had mailed me a copy of a speech he gave after we met.

I AM NOT A GORILLA! I said as I read an e-mail from the author of a book called Songs of the Gorilla Nation: My Journey through Autism. *She wanted to meet me after learning that I was the first African American presiding judge in Denver. She wanted to confirm that my experiences had been much like what she had discovered in her studies of gorillas. The walls went up! Comparing African Americans with animals brought back those old racial stereotypes. What does her journey with gorillas have to do with me?*

I did some research and found that she indeed studied primates. She had only recently been diagnosed with autism. Curiosity got the best of me and I agreed to meet her while she was on her book tour stop in Denver. When I arrived at her hotel another wall went up. All I knew about autism was what I learned from Dustin Hoffman in the movie "Rain Man." What did we have in common? I pondered.

She greeted me warmly, and she took me on a journey into humanness. Dawn told me about her childhood. I learned how she felt isolated, unable to relate to or connect socially with others. She dropped out of School at age 16 and lived on the streets of Seattle. One day, dawn stumbled into the zoo and sat in front of the glass window of the gorilla habitat. A gorilla man looked at Dawn from the back of the habitat. In a slow, powerful way he walked straight at her and put his huge forehead near hers through the viewing glass, stood there for a minute and then walked away. For the first time she connected, not only with the gorilla, but with her humanness. She began her journey to wholeness knowing that with the gorillas she had more similarities than differences.

When I think of all the citizens I looked at but didn't see in my courtroom earlier in my career, I know I put up a wall. I didn't connect with citizens who came into my courtroom. The Judicial Performance Commission surveyed these people to evaluate judges' performances. Responses to my survey said I made people feel isolated in my courtroom because I didn't make eye contact. I wasn't connecting with them in a personal way.

After that I learned to take time to look into the eyes of each person appearing before me and try to speak into his or her heart. For the first time I connected with their humanness. That's when my walls came down and I began my journey.

I realized that Dawn's journey has everything to do with me, and maybe with you. What walls have you built in your life? Will it take a gorilla to take down your walls?

Then Beau did something moving, astonishing. He shouted,

"I *AM* A GORILLA!"

He ended his speech by pounding on his chest. Some people might imagine how odd his audience could have thought he was, crazy wild, reverting. Insulting dark skinned people. But I somehow knew that they had seen him in all his dark and powerful glory, magnified for a moment by the attending spirit of all the gorilla men who had ever lived and died for their loved ones, their communities, for justice. I wept with joy and with pride.

In another letter, a friend tried to cheer me about the state of gorilla captivity by sharing her conviction that within ten years an ape would appear before the Supreme Court to demand her or his rights to personhood…and win. I thought about ten slow-moving years, and the fact that the most important criterion for personhood is that people in power say that you are a person. I hope Beau is on the bench of the Supreme Court ten years from now, passing judgment.

Passing Between

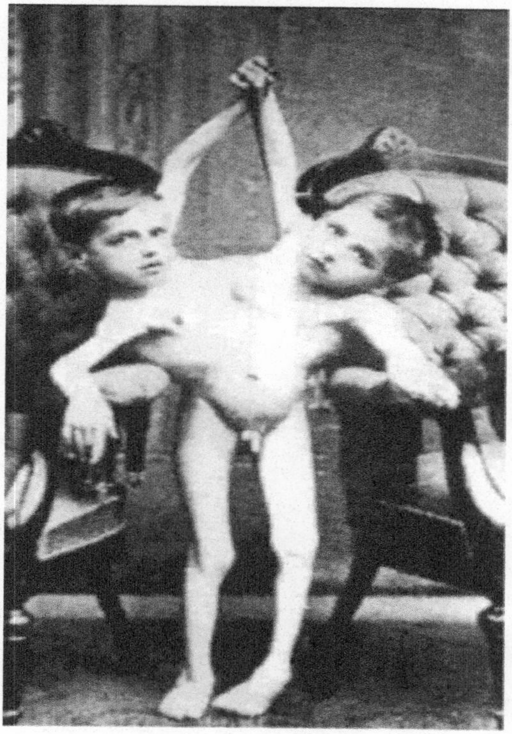

The Song of the Two-Headed Nightingale Child and the Lament of One Body

"We don't necessarily discriminate. We simply exclude certain types of people."

Colonel Gerald Wellman, ROTC instructor

Is it nothing to you, all ye who passe by?

Lamentations 1. 12, 1611

Boston is a city of inescapable connections and inescapable opposites. I looked down the street and toward the water. It felt here like one always has one foot in the street and one foot in the ocean, one foot in history and one foot in a time that has forgotten everything, one hand on a certainty of knowing and the other hidden in an empty pocket, clutching uncertainly at possible loss.

It was the homeless, more than any other feature of the city, that filled my attention. I had been homeless before, and I knew how cold this cold could be, how hungry the restaurant-lined streets could make you, how a person would never believe that an entire city of human beings could suddenly not see you. These things are a grave meanness most people never know. It is hard for most people to connect to those experiences.

This was a city of haves and have-nots, the educated and those who walk out of their minds, the drinkers who drink to forget they are on the streets and the drinkers who drink to forget their fellow drinkers. Everyone seemed as if they are in the process of trying to shake it loose; full of memory, they wandered aimlessly through these streets, schizophrenic, speaking to few--or none.

There were remembrances everywhere, bouncing off one another like one-sided conversations: the rich cannot avoid the poor in their dreams, the poor dream of flying away. I could remember my own past there, sewn to my hip, its wounds still fresh, it made me want to fly away.

But my feet were solid on the dirty street as I looked toward a bay where I wished all unclean things could sail away. I knew Boston would agree to banish all that populate my ship of forgetting, afraid of leaving them to judgment. It is dark under the light, guilty under its justice, shown clearly by what it hides.

The streets remained silent. *Is there any connection left to us?* I was silent, too. Though I waited for an answer, there was none forthcoming. Boston stayed silent about so many things.

As with all the cities I visited on my book tour I studied Boston before I went there. I didn't study the surface history, the grand history -- I looked for its silent history. Lurking in that silence were disturbing incongruities. After leaving Denver the idea of race was on my mind, and certain things caught my attention. For example, the Harvard branch of the Ku Klux Klan was founded in 1921. Although images of burning crosses and hooded men on horseback spring to mind, the Ku Klux Klan on the Harvard campus was unobtrusive, and perhaps more sinister for that. On October 22, 1923, the *Crimson* published an article by the leader of the Harvard branch, detailing the Klan's intentions for a membership drive. "The Harvard Ku Klux Klan has only been waiting for the favorable moment to show its strength, and now there are indications that the next few weeks will see the largest drive for Klan membership yet."

Though the university made little mention of racist-organized student activities, others kept a close eye, hearing what was in the silence, what passed through the darkness. In 1922, W.E.B. DuBois made noise about Harvard's President Lowell who, when asked by black leaders to decry the ugly practice of lynching, did not even acknowledge the call. DuBois' words were left hanging, twisting in the wind.

The following year the *New York Times*, *Negro World*, the *Defender*, and *Crisis* newspapers broke the story of President Lowell's complete support for the exclusion of blacks from Harvard's freshman dormitories. Two months passed before the University agreed to end the long-standing policy. Soon after, as Hitler gained power in Germany, the Nazi warship Karlsruhe stopped at the port of Boston and Harvard invited its crew to a ball.

Harvard University nurtured a close and warm relationship with Nazi Germany through the 1930s, long after Americans became aware of the persecution of the Jews. Even after the University of Heidelberg had expelled all its Jewish professors and students, Harvard sent delegates to celebrate the German university's 1936 anniversary. Harvard continued to be disconnected and unmoved by the black and secret deaths of the disabled and disenfranchised. The horrors of Hitler's regime failed to move elite institutions or those who ran them. Harvard and its supporting classes were deaf and dumb to those who were suffering, clinging to a kind of social Darwinism that believed the best rise to the top, like cream.

In *Mein Kampf*, Hitler said "...anyone who wants to cure this era, which is inwardly sick and rotten, must first of all summon up the courage to make clear the causes of the disease." To Hitler, of course, the cause of the disease was as clear as fresh tears: those who did not fit the Aryan ideal, including the physically anomalous and the mentally ill.

Patients in mental institutions were the first ones to be killed, loaded into the back of enclosed trucks with the exhaust rerouted to run a deadly course. "We'll see the country," I imagine them telling the shuffling group of happy, twisted children wearing lopsided smiles as they were loaded into the covered compartments, into the dark and out of sight forever.

Because the Nazi regime's victims, like freaks in freak shows, had been reduced to a subhuman level in the minds of those in power, they did not deserve to be treated ethically. They were severed from the body of humankind like a suppurating limb. Experiments on those with physical and mentally differences were seen as a way for the marginal to enter the medical mainstream. In the name of science, for the greater good, cruelty became a cross these outcasts had to bear.

Josef Mengele, the infamous death camp doctor, was well-educated and, in the estimation of those who knew him outside the Nazi death camps, a gentle man. Working under the auspices of the Kaiser Wilhelm Institute for Anthropology, Genetics, and Eugenics, Mengele expanded his area of interest beyond the individual and into the territory of mirrored suffering, experimenting on twins, who in his view offered the most efficient laboratory in which to observe inherited human traits. Starting in May of 1944, experimental subjects were pulled out of groups bound for the gas chambers.

Mothers, at the end of their unbearable journeys in cattle cars across the frozen countryside, their twins in their arms, swaying back and forth down the long tracks to darker pain, would hear of Mengele's experiments. Believing that they would be spared, mothers fought to give their children to Mengele at the end of the journey. It is eerie to read the written reports that survive of that time, describing a Mengele who was solicitous with the children under his care. Unlike the other prisoners, they were well fed, and given toys and candy. Some of the children who survived these years would later say that they called him "Good Uncle."

Mengele made sure the twins were first photographed, and that every possible dimension of their bodies was measured. Sometimes Mengele put drops in their eyes. The children's eyes would burn and weep pus, and some lost partial vision. It was part of an experiment intended to change their eye color to blue. Mengele performed blood transfusions between twins, carefully noting their reactions. Sometimes the twins reacted badly to taking in each other's blood. Both would sicken. But to Mengele the twins were one, not two, bound in suffering for the greater good.

Vera Alexander, a Jewish prisoner posted to one of the barracks for twins, related a story:

"One day Mengele brought chocolate and special clothes. The next day an SS man, on Mengele's instructions, took away two children, who happened to be my favorites: Guido and Nino, aged about four. Two, perhaps three days later the SS man brought them back in a frightening condition. They had been sewn together like Siamese twins. The hunchbacked child was tied to the second one on the back and wrists. Mengele had sewn their veins together. The wounds were filthy and they festered. There was a powerful stench of gangrene. The children screamed all night long. Somehow their mother managed to get hold of morphine and put an end to their suffering."

Many times, after the photographs and measurements were taken, Mengele would dispense with all other experiments and order twins to be killed by injection so that he could go on to compare their internal organs at autopsy. I wonder why and how he was so singular, so disconnected from their suffering. I imagine him reaching into their small, warm guts, searching for a link, a link he himself never made.

After the war was over and the Nazi camps were liberated, twenty-four German doctors were brought to trial at the Nuremberg Medical Trial, which began in October of 1946 and lasted a year. Dr. Mengele was not then among the accused, even though all of those brought to trial knew about the experiments performed. Unbelievably, eight of the defendants were acquitted. Fifteen of the 24 doctors were found guilty of crimes. Of those, seven were given the death penalty.

From this trial the Nuremberg Codes were developed, "a 10-point code of human experimentation ethics which [set] the general agenda for all future ethical and legal questions pertaining to the conduct of human experimentation." These codes underpin the formal code of ethics still used at every medical college today, including Harvard Medical School.

As I stood in the middle of Boston, seemingly so far in time and space from such cruelty as Mengele's I thought about the tremendous amounts of blood that were collected from each pair of twins. I thought about all the blood that would add up to over the years, over miles of railroad track and vein, enough to put a thin, red line around Harvard and the street I was standing on, enough to stain the red bricks of this city a darker hue.

Wandering the streets of Boston outside Harvard University, I felt I was living in two places simultaneously--in my past and in my present. I had decided long ago never to allow myself to dwell in the future, because I had a premonition that if I knew how much feeling was waiting there, I might not want to meet it. I had a vague awareness that the joy and poignancy, the pain and exultation of it would crush me; so I chose to hover somewhere between my individual memories and the present, in flashes of time that researchers tell us last 1/25th of a second.

It was scientists at places like Harvard that measured those things and I, like most people, didn't have time to check and see if their calibrations were accurate. Others, like the homeless people around me on the streets, measured time differently—in seconds until the warmer sun emerged from cold night, in minutes until eating, in days away from home, in lost years that are so similar to each other that you can think of them all in the span of now.

Time flies when you're having fun, I thought as I walked by a homeless man shining shoes. The customer standing with his foot on the rough shoeshine box looked over the homeless man's head, as if he just happened to have a man attached to his shoe.

Stopping to look in the window of an expensive shop, I saw reflected in the glass the image of a homeless man pushing a cart. He held a bottle, his elixir. People moved out of his way: people dressed for work, people going to their classes, a young man with a tee-shirt that read *College: We drink more before 9 a.m. than most people drink in a day!* Another tee-shirt, on a young woman, read *8 out of 10 of the voices in my head say "Don't shoot!"* They didn't look at the man with a cart, not because they didn't care; I believed it is because this man, and other people living outside, reminded people that we are all animals. The wild-living people on the streets make them afraid that they could be stalked and bitten, toothed up and scratched out, here where nothing is predictable.

I continued to watch the reflections in the glass. As they moved by I reflected on a 53-year-old homeless man I read about who lived in subway stations in New York, who read philosophy, played chess, and announced system route changes or delays. He didn't drink or take drugs; he wasn't crazy. Tony – most people didn't know his name until he died – never knew his father. When he was 18, he saw his mother murdered during a robbery. Alone, he drifted. He played chess well enough to make a living at city parks. He was afraid of shelters and lived in the subway instead, where rats and steel dust shaved years off his life.

People who talked to him opened up, drawing a more positive perspective from his kindness. He had many friends who brought him food and money. He gave them back advice about life. "Wrong is what makes the world go around," he said.

A motorman who knew Tony for fifteen years said, "When you go outside, most people stay in their socioeconomic circle, their own racial circle. When you go outside that circle, you're taking a chance. You can find rejection, or you can be enlightened." Tony once told someone that he saw himself as a beacon of freedom.

As I watched the reflections gliding by in the window, I felt connected to all of them. Each and every one. That was part of what I had been told was a disability, my disability that made it impossible for me to get a job, the disability that led to my own homelessness. A mental illness, like the ones so many homeless people have, a mental illness that I have been told again and again makes me separate.

"People with autism are disconnected," people tell me, as if to make sure I get it right. "They just can't connect with others. They don't have empathy like normal people do. Something is just missing in them." They say it like they are giving a well-rehearsed speech in front of a mirror.

Through my disability I felt like I was the young woman that was hurrying to her class in economics; I felt that the old professor with his pipe and corduroy jacket was me, that the woman stopping to give the homeless man some money was me -- a passer-by giving an offering to anyone who would take it. And I felt that the homeless man was me, too. I felt conjoined to them all at the heart, warm sweet blood between us.

Sweetness. I tried to think of a sweet story I had read about Boston. I thought of one. Unfortunately, my mind works in an unusual way, both literal and associative.

In 1919, on a cold January day, a low rumble of warning came from the Purity Distilling Company in Boston's North End. An enormous vat of molasses burst, and a wall of sticky sweetness poured down Commercial Street. The wave of molasses was two stories high, and it washed over and tied together everything in its path. As if in defiance of the saying "As slow as molasses in January," the tidal force swept quickly over everything in its path. People on the street couldn't outrun the immense black wave, and were engulfed in two million gallons of molasses. Twenty-one people either drowned or suffocated, and another 150 people were injured. The police had to shoot horses, one by one, that were trapped in the mire. Boston Harbor was brown until summer, and the city itself smelled like molasses for weeks. Just the smell of that sweetness must have brought tears to survivors for years. I imagined all the people who could never eat baked beans again.

The molasses had been destined for rum. In the reflection of the window I saw the homeless man drinking from his brown paper bag. We were destined to be thick, to be bound together, and this time, in the bottle he held, the molasses fulfilled its destiny. My focus on the window blurred, and for a moment I become the window, too, and the images beyond it.

I saw the print of a blackbird in the store window, and I let my thoughts return to the folio I carried with pictures of freaks in it. Next to my picture of the spotted human Leopard Boy are two portraits I have of the Leopard Girl, the black and white African child that had been exhibited in Europe in the 1700s. In both frames of her pictures she held a little bird in her hand. Was it to remind us of her nature, her fragility? Was it to remind us that she came in many colors? I don't know. I imagine people walking by, pretending not to see her, or people feeling sorry for her and pressing money into her tiny hand, her hand itself like a small wing, black and white. Maybe she sang. Maybe that is what connected her to people.

I had been reading about a pair of singing black twins who were joined at the base of the spine, separate upper bodies joined below the waist. She was called Millie Christine, one name for one person. Her family always referred to her as "the baby," "the child," as "sister." They called her the Two-Headed Nightingale because she sang so beautifully.

Everyone said that Millie Christine was unusually intelligent and sensitive. She amazed people when one head of the nightingale would sleep and the other would be wide awake. Born in North Carolina in 1851 to Monemia McKoy, the twins came into the world as slaves. In 1852, when Millie Christine was ten months old, she was bought by speculators for a thousand dollars. Through the years she changed hands many times, but always she was shown to the public, that disconnected crowd that longs for the singular experience. The advertising bill read:

GREAT ATTRACTION!
THE CELEBRATED CAROLINA TWINS
will be exhibited at Raleigh during the agricultural fair.
These children have been pronounced by Physicians the
most interesting specimen of humanity ever seen…
Many Physicians have examined them, and all agree
in their being the greatest curiosity ever heard of…

In the spring of 1855, a Professor Millar was conducting class at the college which he had founded, City Commercial College, in Pittsburgh. He decided he was tired of laboring under the yoke of academia, of being tied to one place. He sold the college and, in what was presumably a complete break from the kind of people he had been dealing with in the academy, he spread the word that he was looking for freaks to exhibit.

He heard through a friend about "a strange and curious freak of nature which would secure a fortune for the proprietor," the Two-Headed Nightingale.

Greed is as old as magnetic north. Professor Millar determined to "take hold of this wonderful natural freak, which turned out to be two Negro children…united by nature at their backbones." And he did. The professor found Millie Christine in Boston, in the sporadic care of a black woman who claimed to be her mother. The professor was skeptical of the woman's claim; a feeling that was fortified when he offered to buy Millie Christine and the woman took his money and walked away without looking back.

Several times throughout her life Millie Christine would be invited to Harvard, not to study of course, though she was exceptionally bright, but to be measured and examined by professors who wanted to see her naked body, her anus, her vagina. Later in her life she wrote a song:

It's not modest of one's self to speak,
But daily scanned from head to feet
I freely talk of everything –
Sometimes to people wondering.

Some persons say I must be two;
The doctors say this is not true;
Some cry out "humbug" till they see,
Then they say, "Great mystery!"

Two heads, four arms, four feet,
All in one perfect body meet;
I am most wonderfully made,
All scientific men have said.

None like me since the days of Eve –
None such perhaps will ever live;
A marvel to myself am I,
As well to all who passes by.

I'm happy, quite, because I'm good;
I love my Saviour and my God;
I love all things that God has done,
Whether I'm created two or one.

How long Millie Christine lived in Boston I never found out; but as early as 1854, when Millie Christine was only three years old, she was displayed at Barnum's American Museum in New York City, billed as "the Celebrated African United Twins."

The corner building housing Barnum's Museum was decorated on all three of its faces with huge paintings of animals, and tall, imposing letters that spelled out BARNUM'S AMERICAN MUSEUM. Above the paintings and advertisements foreign flags ruffled in the breeze. An enormous American flag waved on top of the building, trumping the disparate lesser colors of foreign lands. Barnum believed that "Advertising is like learning – a little is a dangerous thing."

The man who would exhibit the Two Headed Nightingale, Phineas Taylor Barnum, was born in 1810 in Bethel, Connecticut, one day after the Fourth of July. I have always wondered, after reading about his life, if he had hurried his birth to see what was going on with all that noise and sparkle, and to see if there was any money to be made from it.

The fireworks being over on the actual day of his birth, maybe he felt cheated or lost a little momentum, as he started off working on his father's farm; but young Phineas had higher ambitions. By age eighteen he had already demonstrated a brilliant mind for business. As a result of his shrewd dealings he bought his own grocery store, using part of the store as a lottery operation. In 1831 he started his own newspaper, the *Herald of Freedom,* and in no time was jailed for libel. Even then his taste for the sensational led him to jump off the edges of truth with delighted abandon. Taking others for a ride-along was also an early gift; when he was released from jail there was a huge celebration by the folks in his town, culminating in a parade.

Barnum eventually sold his store and his paper, a success by many standards but far too small for the possibilities he imagined. He moved to New York City, and got his start in show business when he bought and displayed Joice Heth, an elderly black woman he claimed was 161 years old. For attractive good measure, he added that she'd worked as George Washington's nursemaid. She died the next year. Despite her (unsurprising) demise, Barnum had learned in that short time how lucrative human oddities could be. This set him on the path that would eventually intersect with Millie Christine.

Barnum became involved in the circus in 1836 when he joined the Aaron Turner Circus as a ticket taker. He was nearly killed when the owner, to drum up publicity, told a mob in Annapolis that Barnum was wanted for murder. Though Turner stopped the angry crowd from killing

P.T., he was delighted that the notoriety from the ruckus succeeded in "filling their tent." It's easy to imagine this as a transformative event for young Barnum, who, at the edge of a near-death experience, must have seen the Divine Light of Ballyhoo.

Barnum decided to move on—maybe he decided to dish out publicity rather than be trampled by it—and in 1841, using a worthless piece of Connecticut swampland as collateral, he leased John Scudder's American Museum. When he eventually purchased the museum, it already held a tantalizing collection of waxworks, stuffed animals, and other displays. Taking stock, he added as much of the bizarre and unusual he could find, including strongmen, magicians, ventriloquists, and knife throwers. From a Boston museum Barnum rented the mummified remains of the "Feejee Mermaid," the desiccated oddity that was eventually revealed to be the top half of a shaved monkey sewn onto the lower half of a fish. It was a huge attraction.

Before Millie Christine's time people flocked to the museum to see Anna Swan, the 7'11' Nova Scotia Giantess, Vantile Mack, who weighed 257 pounds at seven years old, and Charles Stratton, the 25" midget billed as Tom Thumb. Later, they came to see Millie Christine…and, of course, the conjoined twins that were to give such twins the common moniker they were forever to be known by: the Siamese Twins Chang and Eng.

In 1829 Boston became the first place to exhibit Chang and Eng. Born in 1811 to Thai parents, the twins were joined by a four- inch-wide band of flesh chest to chest. Local custom dictated that the twins, like all freaks, should be killed before they brought bad luck and ruin to their village. The twins were allowed to live, though, and eventually even traveled by junk to meet the King of Siam, who had heard of their amazing physical connection and sent for them.

Until they were seventeen the twins provided for the family, especially after their father died. The family was always leaning over the edge of poverty. The twins fished together, went to market together, and ran side by side, jumping obstacles for fun. Eventually a speculator with the unfortunate name of Captain Abel Coffin gave some money to their mother and put them on a ship, bound for America.

In Boston, this city of disconnection, Chang and Eng had a successful career until they had made enough money to retire to a small town in North Carolina. Ironically, Chang and Eng, a symbol of enduring union, took the money they made and moved to the separatist South. In 1839 they bought land and slaves, thirty-three in all. They became ideal Southern Gentlemen, citizens of the United States. Perhaps because they felt so besieged after years on display, the twins took the last name of Bunker. They married two sisters from a nearby family and fathered twenty-one children between them.

Chang and Eng toured at least once with Millie Christine after the Civil War, the conflict that ultimately gave freedom to Millie Christine, the thirty-three slaves on the plantation of her birth, and the thirty-three slaves owned by Chang and Eng. Millie Christine gave her family members all the money they needed; her mother and father eventually bought the plantation on which they'd spent their lives as slaves, the plantation on which Millie Christine had been born.

Millie Christine's and Chang and Eng's lives all converged with P. T. Barnum's after they left Boston. They all appeared in Barnum's American Museum in New York.

One might think that being the wealthy (and unselfconscious) purveyor of the best freaks in the world Barnum would be a man without care. But despite his enormous success with the American Museum, Barnum himself was frequently the victim of "mental distress." At 6'2", weighing 200 pounds, with a comical, bulbous nose, he was his own misshapen figure on display, a big top with unimaginable acts inside.

What he really thought of his own inner freakery never truly made it to light. In semi-retirement he wrote his autobiography, *Struggles and Triumphs,* but it was only an advertisement meant to direct people's attention to the smoke and mirrors of his outer life and the freaks he showed. Throughout the 1880s Barnum sold his memoir to spectators coming to his circus performances; sometimes he even gave it away; people said that the crowds leaving the Big Top of the Barnum and Bailey Circus looked "as if they were coming out of a circulation library."

In the Boston cold I looked for people carrying my book out of Harvard. No one was. They did not feel me at the base of their spine.

I thought about homelessness and belonging, being separate and connected, separate but equal… still. Something about Millie Christine captured this for me. Maybe it was something about all conjoined twins from the beginning of time. I remember that I once saw a carving of Adam and Eve on an ancient cathedral. Eve was coming out of Adam's side, and there she remained eternally poised, captured in stone, two heads, four arms, two feet on the rich earth, a fact of union, not the loss of a rib, but the gain of another, inseparable body -- conjoined twins. *Certaine Secrete wonders of Nature*, printed in London in 1569, is a book replete with accounts of conjoined twins. The author tells us that a monster was brought forth in Rome in the year of grace, 1453:

“…wyth greate marvell to all the people of the tyme of Pope Alexander the Sixte, who, as Polidorus writeth, prognosticated the evils, hurts and miseries which should happen and come to passe in the tyme of the Bishoppe.”

The author also describes two young women, born several decades later:

“These Maide twynnes, born in the yeare of grace 1475, are knyt together even from their shoulders to their haunches. They were engendered in Italy in the famous citie of Verona. Their parents were poore and carried them through divers cities to get money of the people.”

The earliest recorded conjoined twins were the “Biddenton Maids.” Born in the year 1100 in Kent, England, their names were Mary and Elizabeth Chuckhurst. The twins, like Millie Christine, were joined at the back. They went about their quiet lives for 34 years together before passing away. When one of the twins died doctors pleaded with the other half to let them sever her, to save her life. “No,” she said. “As we came in together, we will go out together.” When the mirror halves of the living maids were gone, a local church received twenty acres of land from them. In honor of their generosity, the church made small cakes with the image of two little people joined together to give to the poor each Easter Sunday. Connected, communion. To this day the tradition lives on.

On seeing living people thus joined, inseparable forever, people used to living a life of solitude in one body want to know: can such twins be separated? They dwell on the hell it must be to never be alone. I have heard conjoined twins say that it is one of the most frequent assumptions people make and that, in most cases it is puzzling to the conjoined twins; for them, the idea of living "alone," in one, separate body, is what is terrifying. But is some cases, whether because the conjoined twins are separated as babies before they can be asked how they feel, or because of social pressure to separate, conjoined twins do decide to undergo surgical separation.

In a recent example from Iran, conjoined twins Ladan and Laleh Bijani decided to undergo drastic surgery to become two, instead of one after living joined together at the head for 29 years. Both were law school graduates. They knew they risked death during the operation, but then they went to sleep for fifty hours. I guess at least they knew what it was to like die alone, together. Ladan died first when her circulation failed. Surgeons continued to cut apart the nearly invisible threads of brain, but Laleh died an hour and a half later when her life's blood failed her, too. The Singapore doctors, who attempted the separation, thanked the Christian, Buddhist, Hindu, and Muslim people who had united to pray for the successful parting of the twins – a huge, united body praying for a tiny act of separation.

I wondered about the twins' faith, about their burial. It made me sad to think of them buried apart. Maybe they were burned together in an all-consuming pyre. I had wondered if they had stated their wishes before they went to sleep on the table. I wondered if some spiritual guide had been by their side at the end.

In centuries past, when priests were called to administer last rites for conjoined twins, they were at a loss. Were they dealing with two separate beings with distinct souls or a united entity? Such distinctions were extremely important to the church, for if its clergy got it wrong, everyone involved might suffer the eternal flames of hell.

One guideline regarding conjoined twins specified that if they had two hearts they were two people. Another determination was made in 1754 by an obstetrician named Smellie, who concluded that when two children were distinct they were twins, but when joined, they were one monster. The church's general policy was to baptize both heads of conjoined twins just to be safe. *Sanctus, sanctus.*

My escort for the Boston leg of the book tour stood near me. He had brought me here to see Harvard. His name was Jim. In an old suit and a bow tie, he looked limp and apologetic, like his rumpled pocket square. He told me that his son was interviewing at the Harvard Medical School that day, and he wanted to look presentable.

There was something tall and reassuring about Jim; his face was ordinary, not common, but intelligent in a plain and wholesome way, his mind lean and lacking in luxury, giving his demeanor the sense of a hangar, waiting for the embellishment of a plane. He never said so, but somehow I knew that he had sacrificed a great deal to be his own thinker, to go his own way. It took courage to take to the empty street he walked, and perhaps he was recording each echoing step in his head, one great, invisible novel.

Jim may have looked absolutely normal, but in his eye was a reflective window, a storefront from his childhood, closed with all the candy and toys still inside. I wondered if the people he had dressed for would see it. I knew his wrinkled pocket square would flag his difference, I knew that his shoes would show some scuff. The very weave of his suit seemed to hang the thin man inside it, to hang him out in the cold with nowhere to hide, like someone in an old photograph, behind barbed wire. It bothered me to think of him begging grace for his son. I liked this man.

As Jim took me around the campus of Harvard, through empty classrooms and the cold commons, he told me that he attended Harvard as a young man. He looked across the lawn where we stood, quiet for a moment. "I was sitting in the library one day and I said to myself, 'What the hell am I doing in this rarified atmosphere? I don't belong here.' I got up and walked out. I never went back," he said in a way that suggests he is still a little surprised by the moment. Though most people would think he must have been out of his mind to pass up such an education, I felt proud of him.

I asked him if he has any regrets. "No," he said, "I would have become an arrogant son-of-a-bitch." The way he said it held no judgment for those who stayed, just an awareness that every wrong turn in life extracts a price. He told me of his later accomplishments, and the way literature had become a central part of his life. His brother was wealthy and happy, but that wasn't what Jim wanted. No, he says, he had done the right thing; he had done what he had to do.

He took me past Widmer Library. I wanted to see the place where he had experienced his epiphany. That kind of thing always interests me – the ordinariness of such places, unmarked except in one person's memory. Harvard was probably full of such places, of such ghosts of invisible moments. Outside the library I asked Jim what was the best book he had ever read in the building looming in front of us, before he considered it a potential gateway to a personal hell. Jim rubbed his chin. He adjusted his bow tie.

"Anything by Shakespeare," he said, finally. He went on to quote *Macbeth*, with no affect, no irony in his voice. "What is fair is foul, and what is foul fair…Something in the air."

As if he sensed that very air, Jim turned to me and said, with a strangely neutral look like he had read my thoughts earlier, that Harvard had just bought up a huge chunk of land so that it could expand, and that as a result untold numbers of people would lose their homes. I looked down and didn't say a word.

We talked and walked slowly around the grounds of Harvard. Eventually, we found ourselves in front of a statue of the founder of Harvard University. Jim told me that there was a belief that if I rubbed the statue's toe I would get into Harvard. I hadn't told him it was once my fondest dream to go there, but I had given up on it long ago. I looked down and saw the shiny polished metal on the toe of the otherwise dark statue. I rubbed the statue's foot and laughed.

"This moment is the closest I will ever get." I said, still rubbing the cool metal. He shook his head, telling me he had a feeling I could teach there if I wanted to. Suddenly I thought of the subservient gesture of rubbing that shoe while its owner looked imperiously over my bent back to horizons of his own making. I wished I hadn't touched his foot at all.

Jim and I left Harvard and walked down the streets near Harvard Square. Everywhere there were homeless people. I just kept seeing them everywhere I looked.

In February of 1983, a Harvard Divinity School student opened a student-run homeless shelter in the basement of the University Lutheran Church. Decades later it was still student-run, still feeding people, and giving them a place to sleep. The shelter brought together the two extremes -- the homeless and Harvard. A window-washer at the shelter said he liked the atmosphere there because the staff was well educated, people with whom he could have a real conversation. He liked being with people who were working toward goals, striving for something better, and taking him along in their minds.

A big man hawking newspapers loomed before us. Jim walked by him without a glance and tried to guide me past the man. It struck me as protective, touching, and odd. I, who knew life on the street better than he ever could, should have been helping him through its diversions and mergings.

I stopped and asked the newspaper man his name. It was Gregory, and he was selling newspapers to help the homeless. I gave him several dollars and he gave me a newspaper as we talked about homelessness in Boston. He told me it was the richest city in the world and also the poorest. In winter, he said, people freeze to death because they are afraid to go to shelters. He told me that forty states in our nation outsource work for their food stamp programs to other countries. The irony isn't lost on Gregory, who is on food stamps because he can't find work. I told him about my own times of being without a home, without heat, or food. We both nodded silently.

Gregory called me "Sister" and took my hand when I told him I had to go. He held onto it. "They don't care about us," he said; they would rather spend money on war. It is the last thing I heard from Gregory as I walked away. I slipped into the passenger's seat of Jim's Mercedes and he took me to the hotel. I looked out the window on the way there and wondered where the common wealth is in Boston, and in the world.

Alone in my well-appointed room I took out the paper I bought from Gregory, *Spare Change News.* The cover story was about Iraq, echoing Gregory's words. I read about a soldier who inadvertently killed an Iraqi child and, seeing what he had done, turned the gun on himself. Each was nothing without the other, two human beings joined at the spine, one dying because the other died. A nameless soldier and a nameless boy as surely one living thing as a single person. No separation, like Millie Christine. I wondered if the boy sang to his mother the morning of the day he died. I know she will sing of death for the rest of her life, the same song the soldier's mother will sing a world away, the two women now joined at the heart and lungs, invisible freaks of grief.

In the late afternoon I looked out the window, still seeing the dispossessed wandering their paths of concrete and inner dialog. Some stumbled, drinking… alcohol making its invisible way through the veins and arteries and wreaking unseen damage. A solvent.

I reflected on the thought that most people think alcohol makes people homeless, when my experience was that being homeless will make you drink. To give people credit, for some time society has tried to find what causes the kind of poverty that can be seen on the street, but I remember being surprised that it wasn't until the late 1800s that people began to consider a systemic social cause of poverty. After that, it became more common for people to consider the prospect that poverty could turn even the best man or woman into a bad person; but people continued to hope that regardless of condition every human was originally born to soar, that it was our nature to seek the heights. As John Keats declared of winged things in *Ode to a Nightingale*,

Thou wast not born for death, immortal bird!
No hungry generations tread thee down;
The voice I hear this passing night was heard
In ancient days by emperor and clown:
Perhaps the self-same song that found a path
Through the sad heart of Ruth, when, sick for home,

She stood in tears amid the alien corn;
The same that oft-times hath
Charm'd magic casements, opening on the foam
Of perilous seas, in faery lands forlorn.

If everyone could potentially fly, though, then it was equally true that anyone could fall. Since the 1800s people have been more conscious of the road that could take them to ruin and in many cases people have been ever-vigilant to avoid anything resembling so much as a crossroads to the path of destruction. Barnum's own American Museum, for example – as distasteful as we might find it by today's standards -- claimed to be a place where people could see displayed in its theaters and exhibits examples of "high moral value." The museum made it clear through its displays the conviction that bound so many people together: poverty was a sign of personal weakness.

The richer classes, probably trying to distance themselves from the idea that they were vulnerable to poverty and the agony it engenders, believed that a "fatal preference for easy living" was responsible for poverty. No doubt they approved of the tableaux -- life-sized, dioramic scenes – that were staged at the Museum. In the 1850s a wax representation called "The Drunken Family," for instance, showed a household in squalor, its members dressed in rags, looking down into the face of a little dead boy. In contrast, a cleaner and decidedly more cheerful family inhabited the tableau called "The Home of Sobriety." A museum guidebook illuminated for the visitor that, "The moral to be drawn from these tableaux cannot fail to impress the most casual observer."

I was not crying as I looked out on the street, but I felt a moisture. Maybe I was imagining a sprinkle of baptismal waters or the flow of some unseen wine. Maybe I was imagining a sudden searching of blood from some greater body. I contemplated a life in which everyone believed without question that we all had one soul. I wondered about why one person's baptism didn't count for another, even if they were joined by flesh. Suddenly it occurred to me that it should count, it should always count--that whatever one person did inevitably would become a part of the immortal soul of the next person, and the next, and the next.

That night my escort Jim took me to my evening speaking engagement. During the long drive to the venue we had more time to talk, to find the ways we felt connected. We talked about our siblings and the ideas in books we loved, the things we wanted to do, things that take money and time, or time and freedom. As we moved along the freeway he pointed out the broad expanse of land Harvard had bought. I looked as carefully as I could at each house as we sped by. I knew that I would never see these little houses again, nor the people I glimpsed in a yard or a window, who will lose the place they live. We passed by in a blink.

Jim led me across the parking lot, still protective, and found the person in charge, who in turn led me to the room where the talk would take place. Jim brought me a cookie and a glass of water. A woman came in and asked me if I was the author speaking that night. When I said yes, she handed me a copy of my book, and asked if I would sign it.

"I just want to be the first one," she said. I smiled and took the book from her, reaching for the pen in my pocket.

"Oh, no!" she shouted. Realizing she had been loud and abrupt, she laughed nervously and handed me her own pen. "It has purple ink," she said, by way of explanation. I took the pen, nodding my acceptance that purple was, indeed, the only way to go.

"Oh!" she shouted again, "make sure your writing doesn't cross over onto any of the writing on the page, you know, where the title is and everything."

"No," I reassured her, "of course not." I understood. There were places where things should be and places where they shouldn't. She wiped the pen off with a tissue when I gave it back to her, looking apologetic, and dropped it into her purse. She thanked me and walked away, looking completely normal, deeply average …on the outside.

Jim stayed for the talk. Unlike some of the other escorts that have done the same thing, he seemed to really listen, to listen with the ear of a writer, to see with an eye clean of filters, in the pause of a roaming heart.

He listened to my story of loss of direction, the days of my homelessness, the things I had done to survive – eating food out of the garbage, taking drugs or money for sex, wrapping myself in cardboard at night at the bottom of a church stairwell--things that seem simple, like breathing to me, things that seem so distant and uncommon to everyone else.

I finished my talk and began taking questions, ready for the same ones, ready to say what I knew needed to be said, confident now in reaching out. People asked me how I survived my life. I tell them that there isn't any choice when you're in it. It is an animal fact that you simply die or you live. I have never wanted to die.

Someone else asked me if I was bitter about not getting the help I needed to stay in school instead of dropping out, to live inside four walls instead of on the street -- if I was bitter that I hadn't had a different life. I couldn't answer the way I was meant to, because I would have to speak in another, wordless language. My answer would have invaded skin, would have let me knit organs with the people there. It would have made us one instead of two, sharing so much that if one of us would die the other would follow in hours. Instead I said, "No. I'm not bitter." And it was the truth.

It struck me, as it always did as I sat in front of a room of people paying attention to me, that there must be some mistake. There was no difference between who I was as I sat there, on display, wrapped in warm love given to me for succeeding, and me as the homeless person, the eternally hungry; an exotic animal who comes out of the jungle and finds its tongue so it can ask a stunned citizen for directions. I have teeth hidden behind my lips, sharp eyes that see in the dark. I lick my matted fur. But all they hear are words, a wall between them and the outside world, a wall between them and me.

I knew my success didn't make any difference. It wouldn't keep me safe. It's just a show, making it appear that I am inside the building instead of outside, talking to many and not just to myself, able to buy my way out of cold. I saw Jim looking at me. Somehow I knew he understood what I had been thinking. That I could be outside right now and still feel attached by the chest to all of the people there, by skin.

I looked out the car window as Jim drove me back to my hotel room. I turned to him suddenly. "I'm going to write about you." I said.
He laughed. Shaking his head he said, "There's nothing to write. Nothing about my life is important."

I looked out the window again, at the city small and large, in light and shadow, its streets with homes and without them. In the story Jim was everyone who knows that other people will always be more important. He was everyone who knows without knowing that consciousness is the illusion that we are separate, a man with two heads, a two-headed nightingale.

"I see the story, Jim. You're in it." My breath misted the glass. I wanted to tell Jim about the twins who died – all of them, especially the ones people tried to separate.

I wanted to hold Jim's hand, but in my head society said I didn't know him well enough. One impulse felt like a ligament, one impulse felt like a scalpel. My side opened to him and waited for his to join it.

That night, as I laid down to go to sleep, surrounded by softness, surrounded by the texture of having, I looked in my scrapbook of freaks. My pictures fell open to the Tocci brothers. Two heads, one boy, his hands in the photograph reaching upward to other hands, to his own. I stared at the picture, my heart breaking, seeing my head there, and Jim's head there, then my head and the head of Anthony the homeless newspaper man, then the head of Adolf Hitler, and of the students at the Harvard shelter. We breathe the same air, hurting and laughing and reaching up to the hand of others and to our own. We will die together.
We are connected. I answered for Boston. I answered for this world. *We are connected, and that is the thing, the whole thing.*
Everything, everything, passes between us all.

Passing Over

The Endless Cocoon of the Human Caterpillar and Flight at the Speed of Sound

"My fellow astronauts..."

Vice-President Dan Quayle, beginning a speech at an Apollo 11 anniversary celebration.

On the date of my birth, although years before I was born, when time was different and the sky was a veil more deeply blue, a chimpanzee named Ham went up into space in a rocket. He was a baby, still in need of his mother's breast and her gravity, and the gravity of the good earth. But as a reflection of a newer humanity, he streaked into the darkness and waited on the touch of heaven, to be the first person to cry in space. He was little more than a circus animal to people then, trained to push the right buttons and pressed into service for our grave amusement, our search for the hidden truth, a performer in the carnival that promised we could leave our own performances behind if we broke free of the arms of the earth and raced, like the monstrous afflicted, to God in the heavens, our strangeness healed and passed.

At dawn on January 31st, 1961, Ham was strapped into his bio-pack and began the slow ascent up the elevator to the cockpit. The "Primate Suborbital and Auto-abort" of NASA's Project Mercury stood ready to make history. As a small and unsuspecting Ham sat encased in the monolith on the launching pad, alone in the dim interior and hidden from view, 500 human beings from the space program, the military, and industry stood together outside, away from danger.

The countdown was aborted again and again as equipment on the spaceship malfunctioned. Repairs were attempted. Ham sat strapped in his restraining chair, waiting for four hours. Though the problems were never fully fixed, it was decided that it was now or never and the final countdown began. The Mercury Redstone 2 lifted off, kissing the earth a fiery goodbye as a likely screaming Ham streaked up and away. Although the craft was intended to ascend 115 vertical miles, Ham climbed 175 miles into the air, and as a result, was weightless for an additional 1.7 minutes more than planned. During this time, Ham was required to operate levers in response to flashing lights on a board before him. Because of yet another malfunction, when Ham picked the right levers he had been trained to select, a shock was sent to the soles of his feet, telling him he was wrong.

Having endured fright, surprise, and punishment, Ham was also, perhaps, touched by wonder as he passed through the veil and into the stars. He was sent up because he was as close to a human person as you could get, after all: a missing link between us and the other animals, between the earth and moon.

Ham fell back to earth and splashed into the vast Atlantic, skipping and bouncing roughly over the surface, 60 miles from the nearest recovery ship. As Ham waited, still strapped into his chair, huge rolling waves began to batter the craft. Eventually the capsule capsized, and began to sink. After waiting forty minutes, Ham was finally rescued and as thanks for the fruit of knowledge he had given humanity, he was given an apple. It was his only reward.

Ham was excited when he returned to his hangar, clearly glad to be back home. But when the flashbulbs and crowds of reporters frightened him and made him angry, he tried to bite several people. Back in his trailer, his suit was not removed until he became calm. Later still, he was taken back to the capsule for pictures requested by TV crews. Seeing the space capsule, Ham became terrified and lashed out; it took three men to subdue him. More pictures. Flash. Click.

On April 2, 1963, Ham's usefulness at an end, he was given to the National Zoological Park in Washington DC, where for the next seventeen years all he had was a cage and a tire swing. I imagine him pushing himself higher, higher, his eyes closed, trying to remember the face of space.

It occurred to me as I left Boston for Dayton – the way it often occurred to me in a sweaty panic as we rose into the atmosphere in a multi-ton jet – that I have always been scared of flying as an adult. I wasn't scared of flying as a child. My uncle owned a small plane and would often take me with him up into the sky at night, where the blackness of vast space poured down on us from above. I would look down at the shimmering small towns and cities, with their hopeful sparkle sending kisses to the immense dark, and listen to the roar of the engine drawing on all the stories of the people down there. Messages from the ground gave lift to our wings, energy from the hive of life.

Somehow I believed I knew how it worked. I don't remember ever asking questions about how the engine functioned, though I know children are supposed to be fascinated by all things mechanical. It is true that I was always in trouble as a child for tearing things apart to uncover their mysteries. I ripped apart my mother's Japanese fan to stroke the spokes of it; I took a screwdriver to the telephone looking for the jabbering ghosts inside. I opened the cover on my grandfather's oil furnace tank, dropping in rock after rock from the driveway, knowing that if I was patient and persistent something dark and explanatory would rise to the surface.

I guess when it came to my uncle's plane I felt no such sense of mystery because it spoke to me loudly and told me all the secrets I needed to know. Even the things I didn't understand were loud and clear in their way. I just needed to work harder to understand. But as I hummed through the air on an impersonal commercial flight, it seemed that the voice of the plane was always quiet, secretive; its fuel sounded like voices undigested, waiting to whisper death only when it was too late to reply.

I breathed a sigh of relief, as I always did, when the enormous craft punished the runway with a dominant bounce upon landing. I felt myself breathe again as the brakes caught, pushing me forward, panting as if I had been in some quiet labor, working to tell myself that all of this was normal: the abrupt coming and going, an edge of unintended disrespect to old places, the touching of the sky inside a fortress, the coming back to earth with nothing real accomplished except the return of my body.

As we sat on the tarmac, I looked out the window at the tiny strips of grass along the runway, where spring-new butterflies flitted easily in the sun. The azure tops of their wings thanked the sky, their undersides gray and white, offering a taste of clouds to the earth and field. I thought about how plain they must have been before wings, how naked and juicy they were, ripe caterpillars for the picking.

Were they like us, stuck on the ground without dreams of taking off, or did they know better? We who cannot rise have our defenses, though. I read about a tiny caterpillar in the rainforests of Hawaii that has evolved into a carnivore. Carrying a silk container on its back like a soldier's sleeping bag, this caterpillar spins its silk like a spider to catch snails, gluing them to leaves so they can't move. Then it devours the trapped snails whenever it feels like it. After the snail is completely eaten, the caterpillar steals its shell. It carries the shell on its back, a trophy of war, a tank for camouflage. When it is time for the caterpillar to transform, it uses its sleeping bag as a cocoon. Covered in shrouds, it dies to what it was. I imagine its brown body, its black head, changing to something that flies to nectar and does not kill.

The spring azure butterflies outside my plane window perched and patrolled all day, eating nectar from dogbane and privet, blackberry and milkweed in sleeping fields, then laid their eggs on herbs and meadowsweet. Far more silent than machines they talk to each other with wings, moving them up and down to articulate their needs.

In the sign language of the Plains Indians, developed as a sort of universal language to communicate beyond the tribe, you had to use your hands to speak. To say "here" the speaker held her right hand closed in a fist, back outward. The fist is moved up and down in front of the torso: Here. I am here. I made the sign in my mind, without moving. The fact is, there is no way we can move that is as elegant as those who speak without sound. The fact is, we are born without wings.

I gathered my things, putting them into my bag, like a reverse caterpillar ready to leave the sky for the ground. I picked up my picture book of freaks, closing my eyes and letting its weight and secrets still me. It sat on my lap, like a flighted thing with tired feathers. I let my fingers drift to the picture I had been looking at during my flight. A man without arms or legs -- like the carnivorous caterpillars, he had a brown body and a black head. He wore a tightly woven case around his body, pinion-pinned to the ground. Prince Randian. He reminded me that flying is a thing of the mind and of the heart, and that real flying is a thing easier to achieve than breathing, and easier to take away than someone's breath.

Prince Randian was born in British Guyana in 1871 without wings, like us all. People said he had a gentle sense of humor. He was a husband and a father. He could speak Hindi, English, German and French. He was known throughout his travels with P.T. Barnum as the Human

Caterpillar. On stage he would write, paint, and shave. His personal belief was that the body didn't matter if the mind was dominant. I remembered seeing him in the movie “Freaks,” rolling and lighting his own cigarettes, the smoke at the end of his exertions extending like a sword-thrust and then curling toward heaven. Prince Randian’s last show was at a small museum on December 19th, 1934. He collapsed and died right after the show. He was 63. I wondered what it would be like to be a chrysalis for 63 years.

Willa Cather wrote, “Nothing is far and nothing is near, if one desires. The world is little, people are little, human life is little. There is only one big thing – desire.” As all the passengers filed out of the plane I thought about our desires to become more than we are; how the dominance of our minds could make far things near, a sweetness out of bitter yearning. Without wings, we still find what is at the end of the long jump. I had a restless feeling. I desired something, something in the wind or under the wings I lost before I was born, like Ham making mistakes getting ready for the sky.

The Wright Brothers museum was only a short walk from my Dayton hotel, and as soon as I put my one small bag in my room I struck out, heading down the boulevard. It was a good feeling to be alone with several hours before I had to be somewhere, before I had to be with people, before I had to be in the air again.

It was really spring. There was that feeling in the air, the one day you know, no matter what the calendar said, that spring had arrived. When I was a child I would take off my shoes on that magical day and run as if I were going to spread my arms and fly. My mother would shout over the wind, rushing by my ears, that it was too cold, that it was still winter. She wanted me to put my shoes back on, put my coat back over my shoulders. But like something that had waited in darkness in the ground beneath the snow, I would know. And that is when I would break free.

Now I was walking on another day like that. The birds knew it, too, and the flies, and the buds on the trees, and the trees that are made into calendars but never read them. I took my shoes off and walked barefoot through the grass, over the hill, and down to Carillon Historical Park. The park is a replica of a village, complete with lazy streets, a town green, an iron bridge, a covered bridge, the Bowling Green Train Station, a Sun Oil gas station, Locust Grove School Number 12, Newcomb Tavern, and Deed's Barn. All of these were brought from various places in Ohio, and now they were old timers, keeping each other company in the park like aging adventurers brought to one rest home. There was a locomotive called Rubicon that had worked from 1909 to 1961. Dayton Sales was a replica auto sales building, housing early automobiles made in Dayton: a 1908 Stoddard-Dayton; a 1910 Speedwell; a 1923 Maxwell.

I walked past the Deed's Carillon, the park's 151-foot tower containing 57 bells, large instruments that can ring for miles, and then I walked through the town green. I stopped at a wood-and-iron bench to put my shoes back on before I paid and got a map of the village. I was satisfied somehow as the fresh grass clippings stuck to my feet, disappearing into my sock like torn admission tickets. Usually I would need to make sure that nothing was on my feet, that they were completely clean. Normally I would hate the feeling of the grass. Today, and only on this day, it felt like part of me, proof that I had been here in spring, dancing on the awakening ground before I had to leave it again.

I was there to see the Wright Brothers Aviation Center, and I found it halfway down the farthest street. A long house with a cupola, it seemed so small and plain. Perhaps it was built to house the first ideas of flight instead of what flight would become. I decided that I liked this house. It reminded me that influencing the world could happen anywhere. When I entered the small building that was the Wright brothers' shop, I was alone. This part of the building was a replica of the Wright Brothers' Bicycle Shop, so there were old bicycles and parts hanging from the ceiling. Other bicycle parts and advertisements sat in a display case under the grounding weight of a cash register.

As I wandered through the rooms I saw memorabilia from the childhood of Wilbur and Orville. A sample of a newspaper, ochred by time, hung on the wall. A plaque told me that as a child Orville was fascinated by the process of printing. In 1886 he and a friend, Ed Sines, launched their own printing business. The boys produced a paper, *The Weekly Midget,* for their eighth grade classmates. Orville's father objected to its careless composition. The paper had plainly never gotten off the ground.

Later, the Wright brothers built a printing press together using scraps including an old folding buggy mechanism, junkyard parts, and a tombstone. In 1889, seventeen-year-old Orville published the first edition of the *West Side News* on that very press. Another placard, near an exhibit of woodblocks cut with advertisements, explained that the following year the *West Side News* was replaced by the brothers' first edition of the *Evening Item,* which promised "All the news of the world that most people care to read, and in such a shape that people will have time to read it."

I imagined their news, their flights of fancy, fluttering softly out of the corner of my eye. The idea stirred me, made me wonder what kinds of craziness must have existed in the genetic procession that led to these brothers. In their dreams and among their papers they folded and slicked, measured their madness, and tooled their trust in the sky.

After the brothers had successfully flown a glider in 1902, like butterflies emerging from a cold winter they felt confident they could build a machine-powered airplane. They wrote to automobile and motor builders, asking them if they could supply the brothers with a motor that would not weigh more than two hundred pounds. Most of the companies answered that they were too busy for such nonsense, so the brothers decided to build the motor they needed themselves.

In just six weeks, the Wright brothers had a workable motor up on a block and were testing its power. The following year they found a way to take to the sky. Their first flight took place at Kitty Hawk, North Carolina, on December 17th, 1903. It was a gray, bone-chilling day on the flat sand, where the wind never slept. There were trees there to remind humanity of the heights we used to live in, but no Garden of Eden.

Orville lay in a swinging nest beneath the 40-foot wingspan, and as Wilbur released the holding cable and held on to the end of the right wing, the Flyer pushed into the wind. Five people looked on. One of them, a patrolman with the Coast Guard, took the historic picture of the Flyer lifting into the sky like a thin, white dragonfly, with Wilbur in the right corner of the grainy photograph seeming to freeze as he realized he had to let go of the plane and let it soar beyond him. The patrolman, John Daniels, recounted his eyewitness experience to Colliers magazine in 1927:

"We couldn't help thinkin' they were just a pair of poor nuts. We'd watch them through the windows of our station. They'd stand on the beach for hours at a time just looking at gulls flying, soaring, dipping. They would watch the gannets and imitate the movements of their wings with their arms and hands… we thought they were crazy, but we just had to admire the way they could move their arms this way and that and bend their elbows and wrist bones up and down and every which way."

Then Daniels described the flight of the Flyer:

"Wilbur and Orville walked off from us and stood close together on the beach. Talking low to each other for some time. After a while they shook hands, and we couldn't help but notice how they held onto each other's hand, sort 'o like they hated to let go; like two folks parting who weren't sure they'd ever see each other again. Wilbur came over to us and told us not to look sad, but to laugh and hollo and clap our hands and try to cheer Orville up when he started…We tried to shout and hollo, but it was mighty weak shouting, with no heart in it…Orville climbed into the machine, the engine was started up, and we helped steady it down the monorail until it got underway. The thing went off with a rush and left the rail as pretty as you please, going straight out in the air maybe 120 feet… I like to think about that first airplane and the way it tailed off in the air at Kill Devil Hills that morning, as pretty as any bird you ever laid your eyes on. I don't think I ever saw a prettier sight in my life."

I walked among the brothers' things, all scattered and forgotten by them in death, like jet trails coming apart in the sky. In a huge round room at the end of the building sat the original Wright Flyer III. It was completely quiet there, like a room where angels sleep when they aren't flying. The Wright Flyer III inspired a sense of awe hanging there, weightless, waiting.

An old man sat in a chair in front of the propeller, reading a newspaper. I walked around to the tail of the plane, God's giant insect wrapped in cloth and linseed oil, a wooden skeleton reaching for its wings somewhere in the memory of sun and springtime. I saw the man's wrinkled face through the taut wires and stretched canvas, as if he were in the cockpit reading a newspaper that the brothers had printed. He raised his face and smiled.

I wondered what it would be like to have my life's work done, to be able to sit in quiet light, in a room like this, knowing that I had done enough, that I would never have to work again. I wondered what it would be like to simply sit, with my famous wings outstretched, my heart beating. *I did it. I did it.* For a moment I could feel it. I wondered if I would ever feel it again, and I hoped so, at least at the end of my life. I wondered if instead of triumph I would experience a life of ordinary struggle, like this man with his newspaper, looking at me across the skin of the thing that flew so long ago.

It's no secret that I can't stand to be around people. It isn't because I don't like them, it's because I love them. There is no way I should know, according to the science of wires and strokes, that this man sensed his life would soon be over, and longed to fly, dreamed of soaring the way he did in his boyhood. But I did know. What was my first day of spring was late in this man's fall.

T.E. Lawrence said "All men dream; but not equally. Those who dream by night in the dusty recesses of their minds wake in the day to find it was vanity; but dreamers of the day are dangerous men, for they act on their dream with open eyes, to make it possible." *What makes us so crazy?* I wondered. Why are people either crazy asleep, wasting their lives in their dreams at night, or driven crazy by the dreams of their days? Crazy wasters or crazy actors, at the beginning or end of life, we dream of flying at the edges of the day.

I walked slowly around to where the old man sat, respectful of being in the church of his dreams. I quietly told him how much I appreciated the museum and the honor of standing in this room with this airplane. I add, though I knew he would think me odd, that it is an honor to be with him, too. I smiled. He rustled his newspaper and looked at me once, then twice, longer the second time. His way of showing that he understood was to tell me all about the Wright Flyer III. I didn't interrupt. Museums ask us to pray by listening.

I closed my eyes, suddenly tired. I knew that soon I had to leave this silence for quiet of a different kind, where other people listen, but I will not be able to lose my wind. I would have to speak. The bookstore would be a museum of another kind, a sideshow of stories, a folioed freak show, a midway of memoirs. I thanked and excused myself to the old man, and left the museum.

There are so many people trying to fly who only sit and wave useless wings, people without arms to reach with or legs to stand on. I thought about all the ways that people are not encouraged to take risks to become all they can be, and remembered a label I once saw on a Batman costume:

CAUTION: CAPE DOES NOT ENABLE USER TO FLY

Still, damaged and warned as we are, we find a way to push against gravity. In 1653 a young man born in Hagbourne, England, was born without arms, hands, thighs or knees. Records said that:

"He is about twenty years of age, he writeth with his mouth, he tyeth a knot upon hair or thread though it be ever so small, with his mouth. He feedeth himself with a spoon meat, he shuffles, cuts and deals cards with his mouth."

In the mid-1500s a man born without arms was exhibited in Paris. With the top of his shoulder, his head and his neck he could strike a blow with a hatchet, he could lash a coachman's whip, making a snapping crack. He used his feet to eat, drink, and play cards. No aces up his sleeve.

A thin girl, Johanna Megrines, was born in Dungarvan, Ireland, in January of 1702. Lacking arms and legs, she danced, skipped. She could pick up pins from the ground, and needles, nails, and money. Her father carried little Johanna on his back until she grew too fat and he grew bent and weary, too old to carry his larval daughter. She was forced to come down to the ground and shuffle forward as best she could on a leather pillow.

A French man born without arms or legs, Pierre Mahieux, lost his mother when she died of shock (they said) looking at him after his birth. If that wouldn't keep you downcast and bereft of lightness I don't know what would. Beyond empathy, though, children laughed at him at first. Miracles happen, however, and Pierre possessed great charisma. When he let loose his charm, the children he came to know at school set him up as a mascot; two of the school's biggest boys volunteered to carry him wherever he wanted to go, hoisting him up, up, giving him a higher view despite his low beginnings. When he was older, Pierre spent his wingless days making children's toys, nourishing their flights of fancy, working the tools with his lips.

Freida Pushnik, the Human Worm, was born in 1923, the year of the first nonstop coast-to-coast flight. She could do anything an ordinary woman would do. Contemporary with Freida was an armless and legless man recorded simply as "Emmett." Although Emmett worked for the circus as a freak, he was also a skilled mechanic. Whenever anything broke down on the circus lot, people called him first. He could fix anything, holding his tools in his mouth. I imagine him twisting his body, an extension of his tools, giving everything he had to loosen the screw, to secure the bolt, to lift the metal part into place. Once during a tornado Emmett flew out of his tent at blinding speed and hopped, bouncing all the way, into a truck nearby. No one had ever seen anything like it. We do what we have to do. It's only human.

After the book reading, I asked my escort if I could go to the Air Force Museum outside Dayton. She was cheerful about dropping me off.

"I'll see you in an hour," she shouted in a lilting way, her heavily jeweled hand flapping out the window as she drove away without looking at me.

I couldn't escape the feeling that she was glad to be rid of me for a while, that she didn't like me. While we had talked on the way to the museum she had brought up that she didn't like the kind of people who smoked pot and "got high." The way she had looked at me made me feel certain that she suspected me of this kind of freewheeling crime. Standing on the curb in front of the museum I felt a sudden urge to chase her car, to explain that the truth of me is more complex than what she had seen or assumed, like a compound eye or a jumbo jet wing, but she had already buzzed off. I was left alone to navigate the open space.

I looked at the long, low brick building before me as the wind, steady as Kitty Hawk's, blew my hair into my eyes. I took a deep lungful of it and looked up at the clouds, wishing I could fly away. It was one of those moments we have for no present reason, a gentle sense that life is floating away, like our breath on the breeze. I felt both abandoned and embattled. As I heard the birds of spring I remembered that the songs of this season are martial calls, territorial warnings from those with wings. We find the sounds of birdsong delightful; perhaps it doesn't bother us because birds are small, and because they are not singing their war cries at us. I wonder if a smiling God hears the cannons and shrieks of human warfare and smiles, as if listening to pleasant trills carried on the wind. Ahhh. So cheerful.

As soon as the Wright brothers knew they could make a machine that could fly, they contracted with the military. Fittingly, the Air Force Museum near Dayton was located on a military base. There were soldiers everywhere in this museum dedicated to the history of martial aircraft, mingling with the strangers for whom they would give their lives if duty called. With my next breath I said a prayer of peace and safety for each of the uniformed men and women around me, the non-biological offspring of the Wright brothers, young men and women who might not be remembered a hundred years from now in grainy pictures of their moments of triumph, but who nevertheless give much if not all of their lives to our military history.

I went into the museum, where two old women, softer bookends of the man guarding the Wright Flyer III, took my money and smiled, handing me brochures and maps. I told them that I very much wanted to see the aircraft that first broke the sound barrier. I couldn't remember its name, and as the three of us struggled over the list of planes in the museum, a bright and handsome soldier in a crisp dress suit leaned over with a grin.

"That would be the Bell X-1 you're looking for. It's out in the Research and Development hangar." He said with enthusiasm. When he learned that I was interested in writing about the plane, he went on with even more animation. "The Bell X-1 was made by Bell Helicopter for the Air Force. It was one of a series of research planes designed for investigating the various problems of aerodynamic heating and pilot reaction. Its first flight was on October 8th, I think, in 1954. What they did was carry it up to over 25,000 feet, under a mother airplane." He held one strong hand in front of him, like a wing, and the other hand, smaller, underneath it. "Then they released it in mid-air and turned on the rocket power." The young man lets his mother hand drop and the small hand under it shoot forward, no longer a fledgling now, but a streaking hawk. It made me think of the Wright brothers imitating gannets on the beach. Their beautiful madness was here, in this young man's eyes.

"Under full throttle," he said, "the flight lasted less than five minutes. The fuel was an alcohol and water mixture that burned like lightning." He shook his head, a rapturous look on his face, leaving his hand elevated still, like a boy who had just shaken hands with his favorite superhero: It's a bird! It's a plane!

I played back his description of the flight and the little plane being dropped suddenly, going from seeming stillness to breaking the sound barrier, and for some perverse reason I imagined an immense and surprised bird shooting fire out of its ass. Boom.

The old women told me where to catch the shuttle bus to the hangar, and the young soldier walked out with me to the bus stop. We talked a little about what we did, what we dreamed of, where we were from.

"So you came all this way to see the museum." He said, smiling. It wasn't a question, but an acknowledgment of the fact that anyone would be happy to be in this place. I wished that I could tell him about my life time of flight to get here, to this place he revered.

"No. I'm on a book tour."

"Oh." He nodded politely, one of the few people who didn't want to know all about my book, and where else I had been to promote it. Only the sky mattered to him.

"Well, you're lucky you decided to come out here." He looked out over the sprawling complex. "There is nothing like planes, Ma'am -- nothing at all."

I thanked him for his time and reached for his hand, wishing it was appropriate for us to just flap our arms at each other. He shook my waiting hand with a feather-light touch, put his white dress cap on and nodded to me as he walked away. "Enjoy the Bell X-1!" he called back to me, waving, his bouncy stride defying the laws of gravity.

While I waited for the shuttle, military aircraft buzzed overhead like angry hornets. Far below, butterflies flitted peaceably in the grass. The shuttle took a small group of us through a military checkpoint, over a vast expanse of tarmac, and dropped us off in front of a cluster of hangars. Another tour group wasn't finished in the Research and Development hangar, but we were told we could go into a nearby hangar and see other historical aircraft if we wished. I walked over to inspect the hangar alone, wondering why no one else was joining me. They all sat on the blazing hot tarmac. It was Bell X-1 or nothing for them.

I wandered around the aircraft inside the huge building, not recognizing any of them, but pleased to be by myself. I tried to experience the awe that I sensed in the young soldier who had spoken to me, but it wasn't there. These planes weren't part of my life that way; I couldn't be gripped by them, or hauled away above their thunder.

Suddenly, though, I found myself in front of an enormous plane. The placard reads, "This is the Air Force One that took President John F. Kennedy to Dallas. After his assassination, a hole was cut into the side of the aircraft to allow his casket to be loaded, and then the side of the plane was sealed and riveted." Unexpectedly I did feel the awe, and understood how these machines could fly through a person's life, become vehicles for dreams and nightmares, carriers of history. I couldn't believe I was really there, alone with Kennedy's plane.

I walked up the ramp and inside Air Force One. I ambled slowly through the plane, imagining it soaring under a Texas sun, waiting for its living human insides to come back as it sat silently on the tarmac. I imagined its sadness at receiving Kennedy's body in its casket through a wound in its side, taking a dead egg back into its womb, flying the feathered hope it had once transported forever to a distant shore.

I stopped in front of a plaque telling me that this was the very spot where Lyndon B. Johnson took the oath and became President, up in the air, with Jackie Kennedy standing next to him, her husband's blood and brains still clinging to her dress. I remembered the picture so well. I knew in this moment that I would never see that picture the same way again. That place in Air Force One had waited for my life, knew I was coming, my own life part of a great invisible history, shaped by peacemakers and madmen, and people who fly against the odds.

As I descended the lonely stairs of the jet a man came in and told me that the other hangar was now available, so off I went in search of the Bell X-1, my latest rendezvous with destiny. I wanted to see the plane that was the first to go so fast that it could outrun the sound of human cries of laughter and regret, babies' cries of wonder, of screaming soldiers and innocent civilians engulfed by war. I wanted to see the machine that broke the barrier of sound and embraced a silence like that at the end of life, the craft that broke and then restored the sky's audible innocence.

There it was, in the center of the hangar. I went to the stubby, rocket-powered beast and touched its piercing, needle-long nose with my fingers, hearing the things its remembered silence said. I felt a soundless blue expanse travel up my fingertips, making my arm dance without movement, seeping into my chest with a breaking boom. Over and over, my small heart pounded through the barrier.

"Are you interested in planes?" A middle-aged man broke into my thoughts. I had momentarily forgotten that I was on the ground. I looked at his deeply lined face, brown like soil, weathered like a cliff face, as if he had turned to the sun too long.

"I'm researching the breaking of the sound barrier." It seemed like a stiff thing to say, superficial, like a flight of fancy against the depths of his weather worn presence. He looked sad and distant.

"Well, this is the plane that did it," he said. I sensed there was something more he wanted to say. I waited and he went on. "It scared the pilot to death…that sonic boom." He ran his fingertips through his gray hair, and then reached out to touch the plane before he seemed to think better of it. He glanced away.

"I bet he thought he was coming apart." I offered.

"Yeah." The man whispered it with empathy, like he knew what it was like to feel things coming apart. The long silence that followed between us was not uncomfortable.

"I look around here," he said, "and I see so many planes I worked on."

"Did you work on the Bell X-1?" I asked. I was excited thinking of all the questions I could ask him if he had. Like the old man guarding the Wright Flyer and the young soldier who felt that this shrine to planes was close to heaven, I expected the man in the middle of them in life to be just as in love with the bodies that soared, in love with wings.

"No," he said flatly.

"I bet you would have liked to," I asked in the gravity, still waiting for his remembrances to take off and carry us.

"Nope." The man said. It was an even firmer statement this time. "I worked on planes all my life…and I never liked 'em." I heard bitterness in his voice. "No, my work was just a way to put food on the table."

I suddenly felt that he had broken some kind of tiny sound barrier in saying what he felt. Although he had devoted himself to fixing soaring things, he himself had never been uplifted.

For a moment I remembered the story of Daedalus and Icarus, trapped, able to escape only if they flew. They collected beeswax and feathers, made wings for their arms. At dawn they crawled to the edge of the labyrinth and glided into the sky. I thought of this man beside me; he seemed like every man who had ever tuned and tinkered with other men's dreams, gatherers of feathers and beeswax for others, devoting their ordinary lives to other people's raised hopes, keeping the incredible hidden. Like Emmett, I imagine the man beside me twisting his body, pushing out his air, giving everything to loosen the screw, to secure the bolt, to lift the metal part into place.

I wondered about this man and what made him accept his lost pieces. What is that spark, I wondered, that made some people rise and others stay. I thought about reading Emmett's story and about the other people born without the extensions at their sides. Maybe it was looking to heaven that brought them up.

Ann E. Leak, for instance, was born around Christmas without the gift of arms, but she went on to change the exhibit of armless people from a spectacle to an experience based on piety. A terse, grim woman, she urged people to submit to the will of God, to be servants to His bidding. On one photograph of herself she penned, "Indolence and ease are the rust of the mind." In her pamphlet biography (which attributed her lack of arms to her mother seeing her father come home drunk after a hard day's work with his coat carelessly thrown around his shoulders) the audience was told that she gratified the eye of the curious public only to ease the financial burden of her aged parents. After a lifetime of toil there would be no Social Security to draw from. Ann was their mother ship. Industry was her watchword and an utterance that flew often from her tight lips.

Industry, industry, Ann would urge. There was industry all around me in the museum: machines -- fighting machines. The man who had devoted his professional life to aviation support was still standing nearby. This man, caught between the air and the ground, seemed caught now between being a stranger and giving vent to his feelings. I felt that he was rooted to the spot, struggling with invisible bonds as old and persistent as the pull of the ground. He too, I realized, was a man without wings, a Human Caterpillar. A man tired from helping others fly, from being a chrysalis for so many years, tired from never seeing any change in himself. He was every man who had sacrificed what he could have been for what he was, a man who gave up his transformation for the next generation, for the love of family, for children who had long left the nest.

The U.S. Air Force would never admit to using up a man's life this way, being famous for obfuscating the obvious, for making the inconvenient truth incongruous, for using heavy feather strokes to paint a more appealing picture of failure and tragedy. When a cruise missile crashed horribly, for example, the military had said that it had "impacted with the ground prematurely," and that the test was "terminated five minutes earlier than planned." Their colleagues at NASA did the same kind of breezing over when they called the bodies of the astronauts in the Challenger disaster "recovered components" and their body bags "crew transfer containers."

I imagined an Air Force spokesperson might say of this man when he retired that an obsolete component of the engineering section was terminated due to premature energy depletion and a cessation of viability. They would make it sound like a life wasn't lost.

I wondered if this man beside me would be missed where he worked, where his time flew by and away. I wondered if I quit working, quit writing, if I would be missed. I believe everyone will be missed, that no one's work is in vain, that no one is replaceable. I certainly don't want to be; but whether it is worth a pound of feathers or a pound of lead, writing is the only job I know. I wondered if my words would be worthy of the Wright brothers' printing press. I wondered if they would have seen that words are my wings.

As I glanced over at my middle-aged friend I saw his arms were tight against his sides. Maybe he would have rather liked to have been born without any arms at his sides at all, just to avoid having to work on everyone else's outstretched steel.

I had read about apotemnophiles, people who believe they are meant to exist without arms or legs. They spend their lives in agony, wishing for the absence of their limbs. I remembered musing about whether they all made their livings through the use of their hated appendages, and I laughed at an unbidden image of such a person who loathed their arms trying desperately to take stenography with their nose, launching the crumpled, failed papers toward the wastebasket with their mouth, or someone who couldn't stand the thought of their legs trying -- stubbornly or valiantly -- to climb a carpenter's ladder using only their chin.

It isn't a funny situation, though, and doctors have tried to help these people. In order to alleviate this agony, one British doctor at Falkirk and District Royal Infirmary decided that he would perform the amputation of healthy limbs. The first person to go happily under the surgeon's knife was an English patient close to suicide, so badly did he want to be rid of his legs, to be rid of the extra weight that dragged him down. The second amputation was carried out on a man from Germany who had heard that the hospital would take pity on cases like his own.

When the buzzing news media heard the story they asked the doctor who performed the surgeries why he had decided to go ahead with them.

"It gave me considerable pause for thought," the doctor said, "and it took me a year and a half of investigation before I agreed to do the first patient... I became increasingly convinced that the patients had had very little success from their treatments by psychiatrists and psychologists over the years." The surgery, the doctor said, was "the only possible redress for this quite seriously disabling condition."

I contemplated what transformation the doctor had undergone, inside, where it couldn't be seen. I questioned if he had nightmares of losing parts of himself to do what he believed he must, in doing whatever it took for things to get back to normal. He would have known that if the medical community wouldn't help them, these people who burn to have their extremities taken away will sometimes turn the strength and resolve of their inner convictions over to bigger machines.

One man decided to lie down on the railroad tracks and drink himself into unconsciousness. When he awoke, his dreams were fulfilled. A train had run over him, severing both legs, those extensions of his body sacrificed to the rushing roar of passing industry on its earthbound runway. I wondered if Ann would have applauded his industriousness – if she had had hands.

After spending just a few more moments with the plane that broke the sound barrier I rode the shuttle back to the main museum. In the shuttle I was sitting a few rows behind the man I had spoken to next to the plane. He was singing "Rock-a-bye Baby" to his granddaughter on his lap...

When the wind blows the cradle will fall, and down will come baby, cradle and all. Down we come, and down we stay.

As I looked out the window I reflected on the fact that Orville Wright and Mahatma Gandhi died on the same day, January 30, 1948, the calendar day before my birthday, the calendar day before Ham sacrificed the grip his arms would have had on his mother for the wings that took him away, the day before he was sent into orbit and the rest of us were born into the possibility of endless space, though so very few of us would make it that far.

We have all had a certain kind of flight taken from us, our light bones crushed by what destiny makes us do, our lipless beaks turning wordless; tearless in the unrelenting wind, we have lost a soaring heart to the gravity of duty. Believing we might pass on in the things we leave behind, asleep in woven nests of sweat, we rest one hand on a broken place near our ribs and the other we rest on progress.

On the plane leaving Dayton, I looked once again at my book of freaks, which I had opened to Prince Randian, the Human Caterpillar, once more. I remembered: flying is a thing of the mind and of the heart, easier to achieve than breathing and easier to take away than someone's breath.

As we pass our lives on this earth the ground flies under us and the stars fly over, looking down from heaven on our passing. We can only fly between.

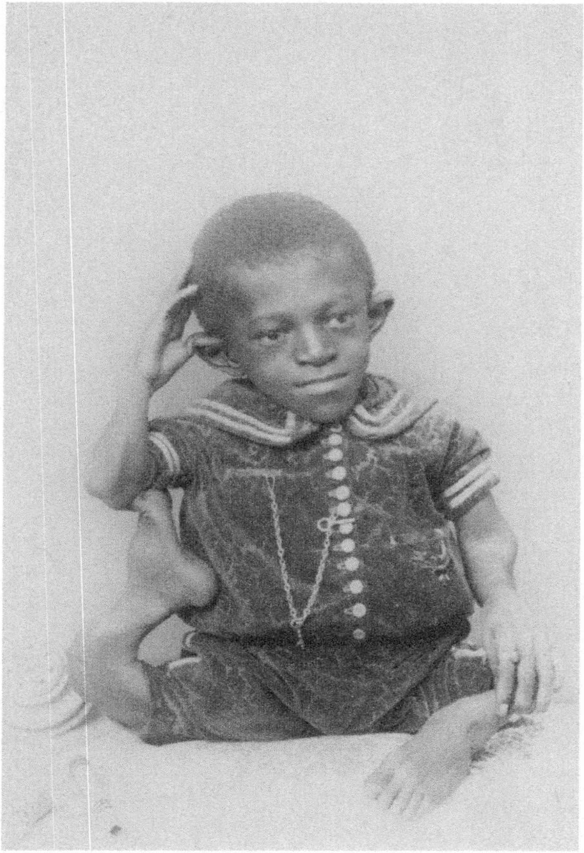

The Tears of the Turtle Boy and the Velvet Voice of Frieda Payne

He syngeth, daunceth, passynge any man that is or was sith that the world bigan.

Chaucer, 1386

On a page in my book of freak pictures, George Williams, a young smile on his aging body, looks out of an old man's eyes. His body is flat, wide, and round -- shaped like a timeless seed, planted darkly many years before my time. Born in Hot Springs, Arkansas in 1859, George came to be known as the "Turtle Boy" because of his shape and perhaps because of the wisdom he possessed beyond his years. Although he looked like a little child all his life, George was 21 when he sat for the photograph with the famous circus photographer Charles Eissenmann. In this picture George sits on an embroidered divan, his short, skinny legs and arms bent at odd angles, his round torso a kind of sheltering carapace.

According to the medical parlance of the time George was a "congenital syphilitic," though no one really knew if the sex that started him on his road to being a turtle also diseased his short bones. Maybe he was what people then called a dwarf, but a dwarf with other problems.

Though he is silent now, George gave voice to his hidden soul as an accomplished musician during his lifetime: when he played the harmonica, when he played the flute and the panpipes, and other musical instruments. In 1889, at the Worth's Palace Museum, he was presented with a silver-mounted banjo by the other performers who knew him well, in a kind of induction to the Odd Hall of Fame.

I had been looking through new books of carnival freaks during my flight to Cleveland, and George's picture was in my hand having just been cut out to join the other pictures in my freak folio. As I tucked him in at the end of my collection of men and women born with too much or not enough of something, or things in the wrong places, I knew he was in the good company of courageous and resourceful people.

I imagined that his voice was strong and I had a passing wish that I could have heard him sing. There is no actual recording of George the Turtle Boy, though it would have been possible in his day. I looked out over the horizon from the plane window and random thoughts about freaks and music and Cleveland run through my mind like little snippets of old tunes.

During George's career one of the greatest inventors of all time, Thomas Alva Edison, successfully applied his wizardry to the challenge of recording the human voice. When Edison finally invented the phonograph in 1877, he launched an industry that changed the world. Edison's first recorded sounds on the experimental machine, scratched onto a spinning foil disk, were a song. It was "Mary Had A Little Lamb."

As I sang the song in my head, I had a sad vision of an empty room with a single Edison prototype in the center, wheezing out the lyrics for all the people who had tried to follow people who had gone away, never to return. It is funny how things die, how things disappear. Take Vernon Dalhart, for example. He recorded more records for Edison than any other artist of the time. Although he was the first artist to sell a million records, he is now a complete unknown, as hidden from popular culture as a turtle in its shell.

In the early days of recording they made one master of a record, from which other records could then be made. When that master wore out years later, the company would call the artist back, and he would re-record the song. Unlike the eventual music culture into which he breathed life, Vernon Dalhart had perfect memory. He could sing a song a year later, just exactly the way he had done before.

In the beginning, recordings were very much controlled by Edison. Later, like an obedient child turning into a rebel teenager, the industry evolved. RCA, Decca, and Columbia all formed recording companies. Originally, the master made for recording was a record, just like the ones sold. When master records wore out too fast to meet the growing demand, the record industry went to wax cylinders, and then to discs made of Bakelite, the grandmother of plastic. With a stamper you could press thousands of records in a fast moving press that not only made the record, but also glued on the labels as well. This faster process allowed record labels to flourish; in the 1940s a tremendous volume of independent labels started up, and the music industry became a booming giant, striding into the prosperity of the 1950s with shouts of "Wop Bop a Loo Bop a Wop Bam Boom."

Fast-spoken words were manufactured with equally fast speed using giant record presses, punching out vinyl 7-inch discs, each with a big hole in the middle, by the thousands. Music would never go back to the scratch and horn. Now racing forward with its memories blowing behind it, scorching the highways leading out of this city to spread the sound across America, music was primed to be smooth and young forever.

As the airplane's rubber wheels touched down onto the grooves laid down on the tarmac, I wondered if music kept George the Turtle Boy young, like the rest of us who let music fill our souls, or if there was some other music, older than we could hear, that instead turned George into a fossil, a stone, while he was still alive.

Cleveland was the birthplace of rock, its auditory wellspring, our fountain of youth. Legend has it that the term "Rock and Roll" was first shouted into the world full-born from the mouth of Cleveland disc jockey Alan Freed as he was describing the Moondog Coronation Ball, held at the Cleveland Arena on March 21, 1952. The lineup included

Hucklebuck Williams, the Dominoes, Tiny Grimes, Danny Cobb, Varietta Dillard, and the Rockin' Highlanders. Like Vernon Dalhart, they are largely forgotten now, but the event set the screaming, raucous standard for fifty years of Rock and Roll culture and opened the door to an endless childhood for anyone who followed it, a fresh-faced heaven keeping away the wrinkles of time for those who would otherwise get set in their ways. Now our grooves would be found in records.

As the car glided toward the roll and hum of Cleveland, I sat beside my escort. We had been in the car only a few minutes before he started pointing out the city's Rock 'n Roll landmarks. He spoke of them tenderly, as though they were his own, markers of his own life, invisible to passersby until he pointed them out, making them sing. Denis had lived and worked in Cleveland from the day Rock and Roll began, and had followed it through its heyday in the city. He stayed after much of the music moved on, leaving the city older, dimmer. He once worked at the Cleveland Convention Center with all of the biggest acts, but remembered more fondly the small beginnings, the Loop Lounge, the Chesterfield.

Denis told me that the Moondog Coronation Ball had only just begun, with Hucklebuck Williams opening the show with his very first number, when the whole thing broke open. Before that first song ended, six thousand roaring kids broke through the doors and windows to join the 9,000 already inside. Police and fire marshals stopped the show and went into riot control mode.

Denis and I traded trivia, his stories coming from knowing, mine from hearing. I told him I had read that Mick Jagger and Keith Richards first met each other as five-year-olds in primary school, and while Mick

Jagger attended the London School of Economics, Keith Richards was expelled from Dartford Technical School for truancy when he was fifteen. Later, the Rolling Stones traded the rights to their 1966 hit "Paint It Black" with Steinlager Beer Company in exchange for a lifetime supply of lager.

It was a fact, I told Denis, that Aerosmith band members liked to shoot cymbals with Thompson submachine guns during rehearsals. They also used to request gallons of fruit juice in glass bottles because of the particular sound they made when the band members smashed them in the shower after the show. They filmed their music video "Cryin'" at a church in Fall River, Massachusetts, where axe murderess Lizzie Borden worshipped.

Van Halen would ask for a bowl of M&Ms, requesting that all of the brown ones be removed by hand. Denis chuckled when I told him that while attending the recording session for the charity single "What's Going On," Jennifer Lopez demanded a big trailer furnished all in white with flowers, tablecloths, drapes, candles, couches, and a VCR and CD player. She has also demanded, I've heard, that her coffee only be stirred counter-clockwise.

Intrigued by my knowledge of strange celebrity requirements, Denis asked me if I knew of any others. Since I had been reading up on pop music and its stars in preparation for my visit to the birthplace of rock, I had some other examples at my fingertips. Mariah Carey once sent assistants to a music store before an album signing to ensure the toilet paper there was in her preferred shade of pink. Then there were the Flintstone vitamins for Christina Aguilera, the mountains of condoms in assorted rainbow colors for the Beastie Boys, the large supply of napkins for P. Diddy with his name printed on all of them, fresh out-of-the-package underwear for Moby and the Red Hot Chili Peppers, and brand-spankin' new socks for Modest Mouse. It turns out that some musicians don't do laundry.

I told Denis that Iggy Pop reportedly demanded broccoli just so he could throw it in the garbage. He laughed again and shook his head. "And that's not all," I said. "He once asked for seven dwarves."

As looked out of the car window I reflected back over the evolution of pop culture and how its weirdness has seemed to grow exponentially. It's hard to believe that it was a relatively short time ago that we were exploring a world we didn't even know was round, a world full of the unknown. Just that short time ago it seemed to take so much less to surprise and thrill. I thought of Darwin's voyage around the globe and his amazement at the simple animals he saw for the first time; for instance Harriet, a little tortoise Darwin encountered on his travels.

Harriet was five years old and the size of a dinner plate when Charles Darwin first saw her on Isla Santa Cruz, one of the Galapagos Islands, during his voyage on the Beagle in 1835. She was one of several turtles Darwin captured and brought back to England to study. Seven years later John Wickham, one of Darwin's friends, took Harriet to Australia aboard a whaling ship. She has lived in Australia ever since. Now, in her old age, she has almost blended into the earth, looking much like a large rock amid the grass and shade trees of her home in the Australia Zoo, where she slowly savors her meals of hibiscus and parsley.

I imagined what it must be like to be Harriet, to have lived more than 175 years -- how much change she must have seen and felt. You can still see scars on her shell where people have carved their names. She was painted a few times by soldiers celebrating coming home from various wars; she has lived through many. She has felt the full force of the industrial revolution: the invention of the engine, the car, the radio, the phonograph, the computer, and television. Harriet saw the first human to set foot on the Galapagos, and she may well live to see humans bring her kind to extinction, for there are only twelve members of her subspecies left in the world.

During the 19th and 20th centuries, hundreds of thousands of tortoises were killed by fishermen. Given that tortoises can go a long time without food and stored water in their bladders, fishermen and other travelers saw them as a maintenance-free source of fresh food and water on long voyages. I imagine those tortoises in dark holds with nothing but time and stillness, dying from a different kind of lack.

Now everyone wants to touch Harriet, to leave their own mark on her; or, perhaps they want her to leave something on them instead. Maybe they hope that she will keep them from growing old by somehow transferring to them the gift of longevity that she enjoys.

As we continued to drive through Cleveland Denis and I talked about rock music and how it keeps people from growing old, making them children forever. Who could have imagined that we'd see so many bands now touring with musicians in their sixties? And it's not just the music-makers who have sipped from rock-and-roll's fountain of youth. We listeners chant lyrics like mantras to a slim, leather-jacketed and cooler God. It's all part of the freak show.

I remembered seeing dwarves, Little People, shadowed by the loud lights of concerts, like smaller, older versions of ourselves. Fred Durst of Limp Bizkit offered a little man several thousand dollars to take off his clothes and spend half an hour backstage naked. Durst kept yelling to everyone, "We got a NAKED MIDGET in here!" Then there was Blink 182, who performed at the MTV Video Music Awards on a stage where there were more Little People than songs or instruments. In a Kid Rock video a Little Person named Joe ran around. "He's in the band," people said, although he didn't really have a role.

Maybe, since none of us wants to be seen playing air guitar with nothing on, our faces pinched in ecstasy, we ask these Little People to do it for us. I had to wonder how those performers felt, if they knew that everything was a sideshow, whether you're big or small -- everything is a freak show, whether you're watching or watched. Maybe we are supposed to think of these miniature versions of ourselves as innocent, children like us before we decided to be jaded and clueless all at once.

Of course, this phenomenon didn't just start with Rock and Roll. Throughout history and in every culture of excess and immaturity large people have kept little people as toys, as the mirrors of tiny, hidden hearts. Roman women went to the *Forum Morionum* -- the market of freaks -- to collect Little People like polished treasures, an enormous collection of faces and naked bodies soon to be bedecked with jewels.

European kings kept dwarves and midgets close to hand as jesters and baubles, secretly seeking their wisdom when the party had gone home, listening to the wise words forgotten by their royal, oversized selves, full-grown adults longing for smaller, simpler days.

In ancient Egypt the demand for Little People was so great that they raised children in boxes to stunt their growth through years of agony. In China the practice involved placing children in a narrow vase with a long neck and a removable bottom. There the child would wait, suspended, for twenty years, while their bodies strained hopelessly to reach a natural size. The art of shaping children into perpetual little people – the urge to cramp and shape them over -- persisted in the Orient until late in the nineteenth century, they say.

The most famous little person ever to live, born in the last century that vase-bound children were becoming living Chinese flower blossoms, was Charles Stratton. That was his given name, although almost no one remembers him by anything other than the name P.T. Barnum gave him -- Tom Thumb. Born in Connecticut in 1838, Charles stopped growing before he was a year old. Barnum heard about the boy and traveled to see him. When Barnum saw that Charles was actually less than two feet tall, he decided to make him a big star.

Barnum told audiences that Charles, now Tom Thumb, was eleven years old, instead of his real age of four. To heighten the spectacle Barnum invented Tom's place of birth as London, and gave him the title "General." As Barnum said, "thereby erasing what little might have remained of his young life," erasing his roots, and making him a whimsical war hero with vague aristocratic pretensions with a wave of his proprietary hand.

Barnum encouraged Charles to take on a regal air, and so with considerable affect Charles imitated Napoleon Bonaparte, David slaying Goliath, and a revolutionary war soldier. He was kissed by countless throngs of women, who longed to hold him on their knees and caress him like a baby. He traveled throughout Europe, meeting Queen Victoria for a command performance. *Just play that old time Rock and Roll...*

Born on Halloween in 1841, Mercy Lavinia Warren Bump stopped growing when she was ten years old and thirty-two inches tall. Her cousin owned a dime museum that traveled up and down the Mississippi and Ohio rivers, so it was a simple matter for her to begin her life as a public curiosity, which she did at age seventeen. In 1862 P. T. Barnum heard about her and sent an agent to appraise her star appeal. Barnum, perhaps already envisioning the future spectacle of a sensational wedding, hired her, and in New York she met Tom Thumb and became his bride-to-be.

Lavinia tells us in her autobiography that their love was genuine, and that the huge show that was planned for their wedding was a secondary consideration, at least for them. But Barnum wasted no time in becoming the architect of the wedding as the premiere spectacle of the times, as highly-orchestrated, publicized, and lavishly conspicuous as any modern big-name rock concert.

Merely the announcement of the wedding swelled attendance at Barnum's American Museum until it was "crowded to suffocation." Lavinia's sister Minnie (also a Little Person) was to be the bridesmaid, and Barnum's other tiny attraction, Commodore Nutt, was designated groomsman. In advance of the event Lavinia sold $300.00 worth of her photographs a day and the museum took in a daily $3,000.00. Money was coming in at such a pace that Barnum offered the couple $15,000.00 if they would postpone the wedding for another month, but the couple kept to their plans; though it was a short time they had been lonely for too long already.

Held at Grace Church on February 10th, 1863, the event was a pageant. Lavinia and Charles came to the church in an ornate horse-drawn carriage. Lavinia was decked out in a long, flowing wedding dress made of silk that cost fifty dollars a yard. A big diamond adorned the tiara on her forehead. Her slippers were covered with seed pearls amid rosettes of flowers. The guest list was "strictly limited" to two thousand: governors, members of Congress, and a Who's Who of New York's richest and most powerful citizens. On Broadway, where Grace Church was located, the streets were closed for three blocks to protect those attending from the hordes of onlookers who had gathered in hopes of glimpsing the tiny couple.

The reception was held at the Metropolitan Hotel, where the couple received priceless gifts: a diamond brooch from the Astors; pearls from the Vanderbilts; a horse and chariot crusted with rubies from Tiffany; and, from President Lincoln and his wife, a set of expensive Chinese screens for the fireplace. Unlike the pop culture spectacles of today, security was not so tight, and people outside the reception pushed and shoved to get closer to the action inside. Charles and Lavinia, the rock stars of their day, were temporarily trapped inside the hotel by a pressing throng of fans.

Soon after the wedding Barnum decided that to make the spectacle complete the Strattons needed a child. Whether they were unable or unwilling to comply no one knows, but Barnum was undaunted. He borrowed a baby from a foundling home and let it be known that the couple had had a baby on December 5th, 1863.

Their baby, like each of their own public personae, was the offspring of P.T. Barnum's fertile imagination, a child provided to satisfy the dreams of the masses. The famous Civil War photographer Matthew Brady, pressed into service as the world's first paparazzo, was commissioned to take pictures of the manufactured family. The photographs were sold all over the world.

When the family went on tour, babies were borrowed from orphanages in each country they visited to make the small family complete without requiring any one infant to travel. Realizing the charade couldn't last long, Barnum squeezed all he could from it, and then announced that Tom Thumb's baby had died.

As we continued to move through the streets of Cleveland in Denis's car, Eric Clapton's "15 Years" came on the radio. Denis and I were comfortably quiet. When Denis asked me if I had much time to listen to the radio, I told him I had been too busy promoting my book on television and radio and keeping up with fan mail from all over the world to do much of anything else. I laughed, remembering my recent radio satellite tour, a unique form of torture Barnum might have invented for his star attractions.

"They didn't really tell me what the radio tour was going to be like until it was close to happening," I explained. "Maybe they were worried I'd move to Europe so I could avoid it."

"What was it like?" he asked, giving me a little grimace.

"Well," I sighed, "Since I was on the West Coast I had to get up at four o'clock in the morning to start doing interviews on the East Coast. As soon as the first one was finished, the Random House publicist would dial up the next interviewer and we'd start all over again. I would do ten or so in a row, for hours, moving across the country from tower to tower, east to west, riding on radio waves. I did that for a few days, getting up every morning for exposure in Georgia, Indiana, Missouri, Nevada, and Oregon. I had a routine where I would wrap myself in a sleeping bag with a soothing red light on my desk, throat spray, cough drops, and tea all spread out in front of me." I laughed again, thinking about how helpful it might have been to have someone stand by with coffee, stirred counter-clockwise. Sometimes I could understand why celebrities asked for special little things.

"It was really hard answering all the same questions over and over again." I told him. In that impersonal darkness I felt like I was just like all the other circus freaks that had stood under dim colored lights, turning this way and that, answering the same questions over and over; small talk, small talk. The circus was the same no matter where it was.

"The worst thing was a man who called up the radio station and as soon as he was on the air, started screaming at me because I had referred to gorillas as people." I said sadly. "He admitted he hadn't heard the whole first part of the interview, but he claimed that he knew my political affiliation, my marital status, and my religious views just from hearing me talk for two minutes." I sighed, realizing I was getting tired. I wanted to go home, away from even the nicest people.

"That was quite a trick, that he knew all those things about me, since I don't even know those things about myself." I said partly to Denis, and partly to myself. I was sure my weariness was in my voice as I said this quietly, barely out loud.

"I'm sorry." Denis said. He was definitely one of the nice people. His apology was sincere and it made me feel less tired, less old. Frieda Payne was crooning softly on the radio.

Since you've been gone
all that's left is a band of gold....

Denis and I sang the chorus together. When the song ended we talked about the funny ways people misunderstand lyrics. Once on a radio call-in show, I told him, I heard a person who thought 'Band of Gold' went "*Since you've been gone all that's left is some pantyhose...* Denis laughed out loud.

"And someone else thought Bob Dylan was singing, 'If your time machine is worth saving,'" I chuckled, "rather than 'If your time you think is worth saving.'"

We kept laughing as I thought of others. "Another person thought Grace Slick wasn't singing 'Feed your head," but rather, 'Eeyore's dead.'"

We laughed a little more, and then it died out, fading as if something inside us had turned the volume down low. I looked out the window at old trees along the road, wondering why their new leaves weren't coming in yet.

"I can't believe you know all these singers I talk about. How old are you, anyway, if you don't mind my asking?" Denis asked. I was still thinking about Eeyore, how I loved that character as a child. I think the past becomes more real as you age, until you get to the point when you can't even see the future. That's when you die. There is nothing to hide from the future. Maybe that's why people think nothing of telling their age on either the near end or the far end of life, but then lie about it when they're in the middle, when it doesn't matter so much.

"I don't mind telling you my age. I'm forty."

"Wow! You sure don't look it." He had turned and was examining my face.

"Well, people always say I look a lot younger than I am. Maybe it's something about not having used a lot of facial expressions that might mess up my skin." I gave him a dubious look. "You know, all that stuff they say about autistic people." We both found that hard to believe.

"Do you feel old?" I asked him.

"No. I felt old when I was a kid," He said, reflecting, "Like the world was heavy, like I had seen too much, like my body was tired all the time. But not so much now. It's funny; I feel like I'm twenty years old under all this."

I knew what he meant. I glanced at my face in the side mirror, smooth skin surrounded by road churning by with its gouges and potholes marking the passing of years. Passion and passages. My eyes drifted down to my hands. All my age is there. I'd certainly used them a lot. There was an old scratched recording sussurating in my head. *Why do we try to pass as younger than we are?*

"I have a lot of regrets, though," Denis offered quietly. I said nothing. This is the kind of moment when he might have decided to be quiet if I encouraged him to go on, as if he'd suddenly realized he was singing in his underwear. So I waited.

"I used to get drunk a lot. It was hard on my wife, and on my kids. I used to run a projector in a little room over the balcony at the theater; I'd lock the door and drink, watching the movies, just waiting for that little dot at the corner of the film that tells you it's time to cue another reel. I was pickled all the time." He didn't look at me. "I was mad all the time. I know I hurt people. I quit, though. Haven't taken a drink since."

There is a knife-edge in his voice, rusty from holding back the tears over and over, not letting them come out. He carried his age like I did. I could see Denis as the Turtle Boy, a man looking younger than his many years, hiding in his portable shell. Regret has become a carapace for so many people who are older than they seem to be. Though I was old enough to know I didn't know anything that might help his regrets, I knew I had to say something human in that moment.

"Change has to be its own redemption sometimes."

"Yeah. But change takes a long time."

My mind climbed the stairs with Denis to his tiny little projection room, where he hid pickled like a floating baby in a dark jar. Then somehow I saw him flickering, his life moving too fast, like the movies Edison invented as an afterthought to his phonograph, in the belief that sound plus a moving picture would provide better entertainment than sound alone. The tiny dawn of mass overstimulation. Most of those early films were very short, since according to popular wisdom people's brains couldn't stand the entrancing flickers for more than ten minutes. Now on MTV, images that never stand still for more than a few seconds flicker without mercy twenty-four hours a day.

Denis and I talked about his time at the theater and the conversation turned to rock movies, his favorite thing to watch when he was a projectionist: *Hard Day's Night,* in many ways the first music video; *Gimme Shelter*, the Rolling Stones on their "Let it Bleed" tour as they come closer and closer to Altamont and the infamous decision to employ Hell's Angels as security, leading to one concert-goer being stabbed and bleeding to death. Die young, stay pretty.

So many disciples of redeeming rock don't stay young, they simply die younger than they should. When Denis pointed out places that Elvis played my thoughts moved from the young man stabbed at Altamont to Elvis, still relatively young, death feeling like a different knife inside; when he fell in front of the toilet, his pants down, I wondered what song he might have been humming then. Maybe some tune from his childhood scratched on his memory.

Denis told me that the Loop Lounge where Elvis and others sang so long ago is now Domino's Lounge; the Chesterfield, another hot spot where all the old acts played, is now the Winkin' Lizard. As we drove by the old building a neon lizard sign winks and stares, winks and stares. Denis told me he organized an oldies concert there some years back with the Shondells, the Platters, Dell Shannon, the Four Tops.

"No matter how old they were, for a few minutes in each set they would be right back there, feeling it all over again."

I wonder if any of them felt cheated. When it started, Rock and Roll had winked at them and stared. What they thought was a promise that they would be young forever turned out to be just another automatic wink; in the blink of an eye everything would change again and the wink and stare would be given to others, and still others that would come after them.

After a long drive Denis' and my destination stood before us. The Rock and Roll Hall of Fame. Mecca. It was a huge silver and glass pyramid of a building glinting in the sun, preserving its perfect youth, untouched by time, deep inside. Once we crossed the threshold it became clear that everyone knew Denis. I waited patiently by his side as he talked to one person and then another about the small, ordinary things that made up their lives. We got in for free.

Denis suddenly became silent, telling me he would be nearby if I needed him, to take my time. I was in no hurry to be anywhere; my work today was done. As I walked by the first exhibits, the early history of our music, I was flooded by an awareness that all that will be left of me, all my walks and works, all my songs and sins, might end up in a transparent case like this someday. My life in a shell. Like George the Turtle Boy.

All the history was there. The blues from the Deep South and its singers, Bessie Smith and Ma Rainey, all the way back to the first blues record ever made, Mamie Smith's *Crazy Blues* from the 1920. Gospel's golden age in the 1930s and 1940s saw bands like the Soul Stirrers, the Swan Silvertones, and the Dixie Hummingbirds give rise to the styles that would emerge as doo-wop and rhythm 'n blues. I stopped in front of LaVerne Baker's blue beaded dress, and moved over to see a poster of Etta James playing the Pacific Ballroom with the Jamesettes. I imagined her smooth, young voice singing "At Last." The song lingered in my mind as I went over to a huge display case devoted to the early music scene in Memphis, close to my childhood home in Southern Illinois.

I remembered my grandmother going to Graceland and collecting Elvis calendars every year until she died. I looked through my reflection in the glass of the case, my eyes lingering on a Johnny Cash record, a picture of Jerry Lee Lewis, Sun Records labels with Carl Perkins, and the album cover with Elvis in that gold lame suit. There was Lisa Marie Presley's tricycle, a million miles from her famous kiss with Michael Jackson on television, put away with other childish things.

I went down another hall. After being nurtured in Memphis and Cleveland, Rock 'n Roll started standing on its own two legs, ready now to go out into the bigger world. There was John Lennon's guitar, still as a wood casket, silent as trees on a windless day. I see his photograph as a shy, vulnerable three-year-old, blown up on the wall, and Paul McCartney's collarless jacket from the Ed Sullivan show. In the San Francisco Exhibits I see Janis Joplin's wire-frame glasses, like the skeleton of a little bird long gone from the sky, Jimi Hendrix's cape, and Mama Cass's velvet caftan with the sun sewn over the heart coming loose. I moved through the displays of Mick Jagger's stage clothes, Debbie Harry's black knit dress with its 2,000 razor blades sewn on it, Alice Cooper's black leather jacket sprouting nails, and David Bowie's silver clown suit. *Scary Monsters*. The things you fear in the closet, even when you're not a child anymore.

In one of the cases I saw an old seashell necklace. I didn't notice who it had belonged to as I walked by, but it sparked a memory that seemed like it should have been a part of George the Turtle Boy's story. It was an old legend about an aged couple who had a son they loved very much. He grew into a strong youth, a brave fisherman sailing far out into the pounding surf each day, looking to the horizon for more, and better. People warned him he would perish, being so bold, so far from the safety of the shore. One day he caught a turtle. The turtle begged for his life, so the boy put the turtle back into the sea. Years later, the boy was far out to sea when a sudden storm tore his boat apart. He was about to drown when the turtle he had freed brought him to the surface; but instead of carrying him home, the turtle offered to take the young man on an adventure. He eagerly agreed, and he was treated to extraordinary sights and experiences in fabled kingdoms beneath the waves.

After a time, the man grew weary of the marvels around him and grew homesick for his parents. He asked the turtle to take him home, but when he got there he recognized no one, and no one recognized him. When he reached his parents' house it stood empty. He heard the faint call of a stringed instrument, and a feeling of dread came upon him. Rushing to the graveyard, he found the stones that marked the graves of his departed parents. Soon it became clear that although his time with the turtle had seemed like just a few weeks, in fact he had been gone for many years.

As I kept moving through the history displayed along the walls, all that I saw struck me as though I, too, was like the Turtle Boy. All of these people, these sounds, the images, seem as though I saw them for the first time just weeks ago. Denis still hovered unobtrusively nearby, like a bodyguard. I knew the feeling I was having must be so much more poignant for him. He had really been there. I felt it was I who should be standing quietly behind him as he takes in the images and sounds of moments he helped create. I wanted to do something for him, but I felt I had nothing to offer him but my kindness, my own kind of deference, respect.

But Denis continued to be generous to me instead. He bought me a little pin from the gift shop. It was a tiny guitar, a glittery and detailed a miniature of the grand scheme all around us.

“Thanks, Denis.” I was so touched I had tears in my eyes. It was not because he gave me the pin, but because he had put me back in touch with something much older than the shiny new gift, like the layer of solid rock we never think about under our feet, invisible but absolutely necessary to our lives.

Denis dropped me off in front of the Ritz Carlton. He came around to open my door for which I was glad, because it made it easy to hug him.

“I hope I see you again,” he said, looking over my shoulder.

“You will. One way or another.”

We smiled crookedly and quickly looked away.

I felt our parting seep into me as I stood at the elevator, alone. I felt like I had met so many people on this tour who could have been friends. Long time friends. Instead, as with so many things, I felt I had to go through a long funeral for myself to make room for new life. I heard the ding and bounce of the elevator before me and looked up as the doors wheeze open. Jerry Springer was standing in front of me.

I shook my head and laughed out loud. Jerry watched me, saying nothing as I continued to shake my head and chuckle. It occurred to me he must get that reaction a lot, because he walked away, expressionless. In the elevator I pressed my way upward with the touch of a button. Not long ago I had seen Little People fighting during a staged Thanksgiving dinner on the Springer Show, throwing mashed potatoes, slinging gravy, hitting each other with pie and drumsticks while Rock ‘n Roll blasted in the background. Jerry’s bouncers finally grabbed them all by the back of their tiny, gravy-encrusted shirts and tossed them off camera. It can’t be an accident that Jerry Springer is from Cleveland.

I read once that little people used to be thrown out of carnival Side Shows when they started looking old. With the illusion of their perpetual childhood gone, no one wanted to look at them; they were pushed away by the same unrelenting forces that encased them in Egyptian boxes and Chinese vases with long necks.

I wondered again if it was actually possible that the relentless beat of music keeps us young, or if there is some other music, older than we can possibly hear, but more powerful, that fossilizes us -- whether we show it on the outside or not -- like George, the Turtle Boy, like Denis, like me, like all of us – that relentless creeping eventually gets us thrown out of the carnival Side Show.

In the morning as a new day was being born, I boarded an airplane and climbed higher and higher, leaving Cleveland below and behind. My breath puffed in a persistent rhythm on the glass of the window, the silent beat of life there, always, until it's not.

If I am lucky, someday I will be old, really old. In a time further ahead still, the music I love will be old and dead, too. It can't go on forever. There are things worse than death. I think about the Turtle Boy, the ancient child who played music, who died young, with old pain and a child's face. We are all the Turtle Boy, knowing our lives are leaving us, moving us closer to death than to birth, looking at our wrinkled skin under our hardening shells, knowing we are still the same inside. This is why we try to pass as young.

We know that ours is a passing age.

Passing On

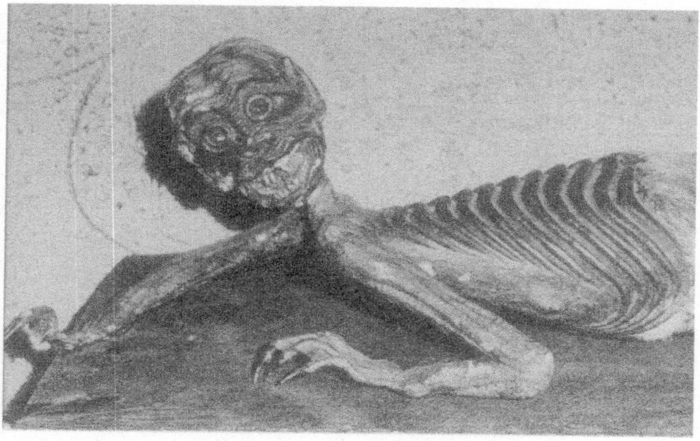

My Grave and the Last Side Show Tent

Sadie wakes up and says to her husband, "Jake, I'm dead." Jake responds, "What's the matter with you, Sadie, you aren't dead. You're talking to me." "No, Jake, I'm definitely dead." "Sadie, you are not dead. Why do you think you're dead?" Sadie responds, "Because nothing hurts."

Last Suppers Served on Death Row*

James Porter, executed in Texas, January 4, this year: Two extra crispy fried chicken breasts, two thighs, onion rings, French fries, fried okra, five slices of buttered garlic bread, a bowl of country gravy, a couple slices of onions, pickles, jalapeno peppers, ketchup, mustard, sliced tomato, one pot of thick coffee and a banana split.

Anthony Fuentes, executed in Texas, November 17, last year: Fried chicken with biscuits and jalapeno peppers, steak and French fries, fajita tacos, pizza, a hamburger, water and Coca-Cola.

Frederick Patrick McWilliams, executed in Texas, November 10, last year: Six fried chicken breasts with ketchup, French fries, six layer lasagna (ground chicken, beef, cheese, minced tomatoes, noodles and sautéed onions), six egg rolls, shrimp fried rice and soy sauce, six chimichangas with melted cheese and salsa, six slices of turkey with liver and gizzard dressing, dirty rice, cranberry sauce and six lemonades.

Robert Morrow, executed in Texas, November 4, last year: Ten pieces of crispy fried chicken (leg quarters), two double meat, double cheese burgers with sliced onions, pickles, tomatoes, mayo, ketchup, salt, pepper and lettuce, one small chef salad with chopped ham and thousand island dressing, one large order of French fries cooked with onions, five big buttermilk biscuits with butter, four jalapeno peppers, two sprites, two cokes, one pint of rocky road ice cream, one bowl of peach cobbler or apple pie.

I keep these kinds of lists in my head – like this one from *Last Suppers: Famous Final Meals from Death Row* by Ty Treadwell and Michelle Vernon -- partly because the lists themselves have so much life in them they keep death at bay. I turn them over and over, and around so that odd things about them strike me anew each time. I notice that all the people sentenced to execution ate meat during their last meals, their last suppers: a taste of death before dying, an all-American meal. I wonder what it is about death that makes people crave chicken and potatoes. Maybe it's because they are as familiar as death itself, as complete an ending as apple pie.

When I repeat this list like a mantra, funny things occur to me, like the fact that people won't touch the dead body of someone they've loved all their lives, but they will eat a strange dead chicken. Or that we will ignore the struggles of children until they are in prison, on death row, and then give them one last crack at good nutrition. It's odd to me that we take such good care of people when it's too late.

I wonder what I would choose as a last meal, and realize I will make that choice some day, though I will probably not know it at the time. The biggest choices are like that, I guess.

When I got home from my book tour, my old friend and college English professor Marilyn Smith had sent me a newspaper article from the November 1st issue of the *Seattle Times*. On the third page, the banner headline read, CURTAIN FALLING ON "FREAK SHOWS." Beginning where I, too, started, the article focused on a bearded woman, taking the reader through the sights and sounds of the sideshow, building up suspense like a barker. Finally the article introduced Melinda Maxie, the bearded woman who sat "alone inside a small tent, hidden from the public like a dark family secret." She worked as the sideshow's "blow off" – a surprise final attraction not included in the $8.00 admission ticket.

In the article Melinda looked back on her poverty, and her memories. Her father had sent her off alone to perform with the circus when she was only eight years old. At first, unable to decide what she was, the circus billed her as "Monkey Girl," and sent her wages to her father. It was other circus performers who patiently taught her how to read and write. Some years ago, the article said, Melinda was attacked and stabbed by a drunken dwarf. The article doesn't explain what kind of lasting impact this had; maybe we are just supposed to assume it's trivial after the pain of the life she led.

We are told that Melinda was proud of the fact that she would soon be recognized by *Ripley's Believe It or Not*. The article ended with her trip to her hometown in Illinois to see her sick father. By the time she had gotten there, he had died. People in the town were surprised to hear that he had a daughter; he had never told anyone. Melinda left flowers on her father's grave so that when he woke up, "God could tell him they were from his little girl, who loved him." I imagined her standing there, a freak like me at her loved one's grave, the sun and grief passing through her like summer in a day, a lonesome wind blowing through her beard.

The article makes us care about the Bearded Lady, about the end of the freak show. The piece stood out to me not only because I identified in it elements similar to those I have written about here – the bearded lady and other freaks, the glory days of the sideshow, digging deeper into important and silent lives – but also because in telling the story of the freak show, both the article and this book re-enact the show all over again. In so many ways the Side Show will never die.

Today, like Melinda did, I am standing in a graveyard in the Illinois heat. A year of travel has stopped here, in the autumn, in my hometown. Amid all the leavings in my life, underneath I have always just wanted to stay where everything is familiar, even the outrageous and the freakish turning into sustaining milk as they become memories, like the summers of my earlier days.

With money from my book advance, I bought a grave plot in Oakland Cemetery. I stand here now, looking at it, knowing I'll be lying in it, strange and asleep forever someday, beside my grandmother and grandfather, who are already sleeping; other people, also strange and asleep in some different way, will be looking down on me from where I now stand.

I look over the ground, the smell of trees yawning in the fading of the year's day, into their long night soon. The light and heat fall and rise, like the dead breathing in unison. The pale grass sussurates with their whispers; they are talking about the carnival of life.

Nearby is a deep hole, a hidden womb of earth aching to receive life in reverse. The smell of unearthed dirt, the smell of monstrous beginnings crawls into the breeze. There is a blue and white striped canopy tent beside the open grave, with chairs arranged for the final viewing. *Hurry, hurry, hurry, this is your last chance to cry*. I hear the echoes in the ground; the ghosts are also singing about the carnival of death.

This is the land of Lincoln, where I was raised -- land of the Lincoln Watermelon Monument in Lincoln, Illinois, "The only city ever named for Abraham Lincoln with his personal consent," says the town. Downtown there is a monument in the shape of a life-size, ear-to-ear watermelon slice, celebrating the day in 1853 when the future 16th President christened his namesake community with melon juice. In Springfield, Illinois, a clean-shaven statue of a young Lincoln stands in the State Fair Grounds, hefting a rail-splitter. In town, there is a bank ledger with Lincoln's account in it.

Charleston, Illinois has the world's largest and ugliest Lincoln statue, now standing in an overgrown and untended area of town. You can barely see the statue from the road; he's way in the back in a hollow, grimacing to himself. His color is fading; there's a hole in his left heel, one of his fingers has been blown off by a lightning bolt, and there's a bullet hole in his right cheek. He stands alone in what used to be a theme park, with faded signs and the jumbled skeletons of snack stands.

A man beloved in life, Lincoln now stands with his legacy in rust, a sideshow. Death makes freaks of us all; it reveals us all for the freaks we were in life. And the land and love will receive us back again.

As I stand at my grave I think about the coincidence that the end of my tour of the nation and my journey home, through Washington, D.C., to Washington, to Illinois, fell on the same dates as the journey of Lincoln's body as it came home here to rest. After his assassination in Washington, President Lincoln's body was transported by rail back to Illinois for burial. It lay in state in Cleveland and then headed west. In Urbana, in Champaign County, the train paused for fifteen minutes while crowds watched from the sides of the rails. Then it moved on.

People say that every April, in the ghost month of my travel in the same direction, Lincoln's funeral train appears on the tracks in Urbana, draped in black, with a crew of grinning skeletons. Halfway down the train is Lincoln's coffin, surrounded by blue-coated phantoms; the train passes silently, the clocks all around stopping then, starting later, and appearing minutes behind.

When I got home from my tour I found a flat, square package in the mail one day, Denis' name and address in the upper left-hand corner. Slowly, I tore off the wrapping paper to find an original Ink Spots album. I placed it carefully on my old-fashioned record player and listened to its haunting smoothness through the scratches between the song and time, the scratches between my ears and my heart.

We'll meet again, don't know where, don't know when,
But I know we'll meet again, some sunny day...

So will you please say hello to the folks that I know,
Tell them I won't be long...

I wonder if we all see each other at the end, as we all really are – I wonder if we see ourselves for the first time. Sometimes I wish we could all dream about our deaths, the sum of our lives, as Lincoln did. He told his dream to a friend: *I thought I left my bed and wandered downstairs. There the silence was broken by the same pitiful sobbing, but the mourners were invisible... Determined to find the cause of a state of things so mysterious and so shocking, I kept on until I arrived at the East Room, which I entered. There I met with a sickening surprise. Before me was a catafalque, on which rested a corpse wrapped in funeral vestments... 'Who is dead in the White House?' I demanded of one of the soldiers. 'The President,' was his answer; 'he was killed by an assassin!' Then came a loud burst of grief from the crowd, which awoke me from my dream. I slept no more that night; and though it was only a dream, I have been strangely annoyed by it ever since."*

Lincoln died four days after his dream. Doctors who attended him in the boarding house across from the theater where he was shot poked their fingers deep into his brain, feeling for the bullet that might not have killed him if they had left his brain alone. They listened to his labored breathing. In the pale of first light, he went out forever. They wrapped him up and sent him to be embalmed, a new practice invented to help ship bodies home from the Civil War, cheating the probing eyes of death, hungry for what we really look like.

Lincoln was embalmed so many times on his way home that when they opened his tomb in 1900, they were amazed at the sight: Lincoln's body was perfectly preserved. In fact, he was completely recognizable, more than thirty years after his death. On his chest they could see red, white, and blue, seeding remnants of the American flag, the fading paint on the forgotten statue of his frame.

At the opposite end, perhaps finding death as friendly as Lincoln's body had, were the *denatsate* of Europe in the Middle Ages, who instead of looking alive after death looked dead while they are alive; who instead of being comfortable and beloved, were beggars next to death. They slit their faces to extend their mouths from ear-to-ear, then removed their gums, but not their teeth, and cut off of their noses. Theirs were horrid visages, living faces with ever-present death's grins and rotting skulls. People passing them by would give them money to get away from them, paying to keep death and deformity at bay. I wondered if a *denatsate* died in the street if anyone would know, looking already dead as they did, or if they would simply melt away unnoticed, staring without being seen.

As I regard the ground beneath my feet, I imagine the ground pulled away dramatically, like a sideshow curtain, revealing the people below me. Some would be black and twisted, some bloated, some like sticks gnarled in on themselves; the Modern Elephant Man, the Human Skeleton, the Fat, Blue Lady, the Human Root. Freaks one and all, at the end our souls shine out of us -- the realness of us, turning our lips back to smile forever, relieved.

I imagine coming here some day, when I'm tired, too tired to look normal and alive. I imagine lying down on the top of my grave and drifting into the ground, wishing there would be time for me to lay long enough here for the earth to take me back, to reveal my true face and body. Maybe I would pick a warm day, the temperature of my mother's body, close my eyes, let my heart stop beating, and lie in peace.

The bacteria that were living on the contents of my intestine before death would begin to digest my intestine itself. Eventually they would break out of my intestine and start digesting my other organs nearby, sending a green stain out on the lower right side of my belly, a garden under my skin. My own digestive juices would spread through me, my body finally working with the earth to eat itself. Bacteria would break down tissues and cells, releasing fluids into all my body cavities, respiring in the absence of oxygen and producing gases -- hydrogen sulphide, methane, cadaverine, putrescine.

The buildup of gas resulting from the intense activity of the multiplying bacteria would create pressure within my body, while young maggots would move in a hot mass through a small world with me as unknowing creator, the mass benefiting from communal heat and shared digestive secretions. My bloated body would eventually collapse, leaving a soft, flattened black slab, reeking for miles as I crawl up into the wind, a free freak with a kicking "k" on the end. The surfaces of my body that touched the ground would become covered with mould as my body fermented finely, drying out; eventually all my hair would disappear, leaving the bones only, the long age of the earth my only afterlife. I would finally be like everyone else.

Once, I saw a postcard with an image of Kokeshi dolls of Japan. Kokeshi are ancient dolls, minimal and abstract. The belief is that the more abstract and simple the doll, the more complex the emotion that attaches to them, like spacious human templates. The dolls look as if through their simplicity they can encompass all of human experience. Their shape is the shape of humans naked, beneath our extra arms, our twin heads, the places where we have no eyes but weep, the shape of finely rotted bodies, the features of the individual melting into everyone else.

I know that long before I would be allowed to rot in my own grave and become everyone, someone would find me and take me away from the ground. Dead and weak to will, I would have no say. I would be taken away and preserved, an odd and pointless forestalling of what I had welcomed. Against my wishes I would continue to look alive and separate from everything for a generation.

Unfortunately, perhaps, there are as many ways to be freakishly preserved as there are stages of the natural way to rot. If you die before you're born you can be preserved for an unnaturally long life, making your way through the carnival circuit in a jar, part of a pickled punk exhibit. Once Thomas Edison himself went down to Fort Myers, Florida -- Henry Ford and Harvey Firestone with him -- to see a pickled punk show run by Lou Dufour, the "Father of Unborn Shows." They got a private viewing, Lou shouting into Edison's old-fashioned ear horn -- because Edison was almost deaf – describing and explaining what they were seeing, as if it needed explanation. I picture the old inventors milling around the motionless babies, old men reflected in a curved glass of a future they would never know but in which they would in turn be suspended. I wonder if preserved babies ever had milk floating preserved in their bellies, a taste of the sweet hereafter.

Like pickled babies, some of the freaks I wrote about in this book were preserved after death and continued to be the objects of exhibitions and sideshows long after they were able to look back at the people staring at them. Julia Pastrana, like Krao Farini, was also dubbed the "Gorilla Girl." Born in 1832, she grew to be four feet six inches tall, all of her face and body covered with shiny black hair. Her large ears stuck out on either side of her face, which was ape-like; her nose, flat and broad, sat unapologetically in the middle of her features. To chew on her fate she had two sets of teeth in her small mouth.

Her manager, a man named Lent, grew rich with Julia, giving nothing up. Being gracious, Julia gave much to the poor; and between the giving, she sung sweetly and danced gracefully. But Lent made her lead a cloistered life, believing if people saw too much of her, her shock value would dissipate. So she read of places and people outside her world, smiling seldom, always melancholy. Giving it all up for Lent, her one joy in life came from marrying him. Lent, she said, "Loves me for my own sake."

When Julia died in 1860, of a broken heart it is said, because her baby son, a miniature of his mother, died thirty-six hours after he was born, Lent had both of them mummified and placed in a glass case. He resumed the tour, nearly uninterrupted. I remember seeing a photograph of a mummified, bearded lady in a tall glass case, her beard dull against the blades of light falling between the inside and the outside, cutting her off, reflecting her past and her eternity.

Considered apes or savages, like Krao and Julia, there are black Africans stuffed with spears in hand, desiccated in newer deserts and dry jungles, trapped in lobbies and museums, gathering white dust.

Chang and Eng, the original "Siamese Twins" died after Chang passed over first, passively lying next to his brother as Eng's heart drew the death of poisoned blood and grief into him over hours, finally taking him, too, in the dawning hours of January 17th, 1874. Casts were then taken of their bodies for permanent display at the Mutter Museum in Philadelphia.

When one wing of Two-Headed Nightingale Millie Christine died on October 8th in 1912, the other waited to say goodbye to the world for a day, time enough for church service after church service, a day in the life of Jesus' faith. Surrounded by comfort and family, she crossed over singing hymns. *I'll fly away...*

Some of those I wrote about in this book died quietly forgotten, poor and invisible. On the morning of July 15th, 1883, Charles Stratton, Barnum's Tom Thumb, suffered a stroke and died. The jewels and horses and yachts gone, he left behind $16,000.00. His wife Lavinia went home and tended a general store until she died at the age of seventy-eight. Grace McDaniels, the Mule-Faced Woman, died in 1958, after her handsome son had grown up to become a troubled alcoholic who squandered her money and broke her heart.

Heaven needs no knife to kill, the Chinese say. As I stand in the cemetery I contemplate heaven. The only heaven I can conceive of is a time and place in which I can be loved for who I am without my mask. I don't want to die without being seen. In my soul, like the populated ground on which I stand, I hear voices that make me believe that people want three things only: to be loved for who they are, to give something of worth, and to be remembered when they are dead. This is the great human secret we seldom whisper in life, in small life, between our eating bread and laughing.

The ways we pass as things we aren't keeps us from having any of our three deepest wishes granted. We can't be loved for who we are because we hide ourselves, knowing we are freaks; we can't give our real gifts because we are often too afraid; and because no one knows who we are or what we can give, we are afraid to die, knowing we can't be truly remembered.

As balm for the husk we tell ourselves we are secretly special -- that we won't die. Perhaps we believe that if we split everyone off from us we will be unique, special enough to live forever. As writer William Saroyan said, as his last words, "Everybody's got to die, but I always thought an exception could be made in my case." There have been none so far.

I wonder if I would come back and haunt the people who missed the point of me, still aching in other dimensions to be seen, to be seen deeply, haunting with deep meaning and no meaning at all. Maybe I would haunt the people who I believe didn't miss the point of me. In this case I think about all the people I have known – many who I met on my tour across the country and wrote about in these pages…normal seeming on the outside, their secret lives hidden behind tattered velvet curtains.

The people I wrote about -- people of different colors, different shapes, different ages, different means, different appearances and different lives – they might love my ghost.

Some of the people I would haunt for love would be people I have known a long time: my friend the professor, who shuffles playing cards whenever he is nervous, winking at the king of diamonds; my friend the writer, who feverishly laid out a garden containing all the plants Shakespeare ever mentioned in his works, while battling constant voices in her head and seeing herself in the nodding lilies turning from bane; or a friend of mine in publishing, who went crazy in public and smashed the back of a porcelain toilet, holding it high over her head like a stone tablet before she let it fly to the ground. Thou shalt not be normal.

A sudden wind blows over the grounds of the cemetery and I look for the faces of the people I know in clouds overhead, in the grass. In the emptiness, it looks like the fairground after the show has gone, the tent nearby waiting for the carnival to come again. The graves of my grandparents, of all the generations of my family for a hundred years, wait for me to join them. They wait for me to see the faces of everyone, everywhere.

I described my family's oddities in my first book, the book that was the basis for the publicity tour I wrote of in this one, citing them as support for the case that autism runs in my family. Now I see that any of the people I have loved, framed the right way, could have been freaks in a sideshow.

They lay here all around me in this cemetery. My uncle could have been the Human Computer, carrying out pi to 300 places, or he could have been the Strong Man – he used to lift me and my sister up as teenagers, one on each arm, until we were even with his handlebar mustache. My aunt Bessie, just over the hill from where I stand, could have been the Bearded Woman. My grandmother, buried two steps to my left, could have been a midget or a Fat Lady -- she was wider around at one point than she was tall, at four feet ten inches and several hundred pounds. My aunt May, who existed on cigarettes and coffee for the thirty years I knew her, could have been the Human Skeleton. My grandfather, born on Christmas Eve, the kind of person to see the face of Jesus in something ordinary, to see the faces of the people he loved in the oddities of the world between breakfast and evening: he could have been the Armless Wonder after his stroke, his lifeless blue hand and stiff fingers pointing out that not being able to hide his difference from other people would kill him.

As I turn to leave this place, the wind blows against my body, making me weave a shadow on my final resting place, and I know that finally not being able to hide will kill me, too. It will kill all of us. When the outside finally matches the inside, when we are worthy of facing the hidden reward, we will go. Then there is a farther fair, a fairer end; we will pass beyond our hiding.

I think about leaving my scrapbook here, my photographic collection of oddities, the words and pictures of the freaks that made me understand that no one is a freak, that everyone is a freak. I find I can't leave it behind. I need to have it with me as I pass along.

Our world is a freak show, our tiny images flickering past and disappearing, making us delightfully ugly, this is the thing that binds us at the belly, makes us want to come out of our shells and spot each other in the shadows, each of us missing links to each other, reaching out with the vulnerable poignancy of ancient statues, their arms broken away, unable to embrace, but able to endure.

This is our circus of souls.

Passing Press

The Blow Off

"Fiction writing is great; you can make up almost anything!"
-Ivana Trump, on finishing her first novel

Many years ago, when P.T. Barnum's American Museum was in its heyday, Barnum placed enticing signs outside each exhibit: *THIS WAY TO THE EGRESS*.... Museum-goers' interest and excitement built as they neared the promised egress – was it a rare snowy bird from some distant land? Was it a freak beyond description? Of course, as they would inevitably find out, the "egress" was just a way out of the museum.

I am no stranger to disappointing the audience at the end of the day. Once, during the tour, a young man asked me excitedly, "Are you one of those idiot savants who can figure things out? You know, those people that are, like, math wizards and stuff?" I expected him to drop a box of toothpicks any moment, expecting me to give him the exact number of the spilled fragments of wood at a glance.

"No." I said. "I am the kind of idiot savant that can't balance my checkbook, but I am really brilliant about other kinds of things; for instance I know that no one likes to be called an idiot."

"Oh," he said, clearly disappointed. "I guess that's not your fault."

"Well, we can only try our best, can't we?" I answered. He walked away.

You have passed the freak show. Here I offer you an egress, but my aim is to do better than P.T. Barnum, to promise less and deliver more.

When I first started this book, I wanted to call it *Hating Everyone: A Compassionate Guide.* Now that I have seen that no one is normal, I know that there is a shadow waiting to be born, waiting to whisper the great human secret. It is a shadow in need of peace, a shadow beyond love or hate. Strangeness isn't a personal matter, a set of characteristics that one person has – or doesn't have; oddity is found in the way we think about and present people. As Barnum and Bailey's sideshow manager Clyde Ingalls said, "Freaks are what you make them. Take any peculiar-looking person, whose familiarity to those around him makes for acceptance, play up that peculiarity and add a good spiel and you have a great attraction." I feel like I have been a successful freak in just this way.

There are hundreds of books on autism now, but because we are all so different, I only see an occasional puff of smoke shaped like me drift across their pages. I have seen such an apparition of myself in the Diagnostic and Statistical Manual, Forth Edition, under the criteria for Asperger's Syndrome: *Qualitative impairment in social interaction...marked impairments in the use of multiple nonverbal behaviors such as facial expression...body postures, and gestures, to regulate social interaction... lack of seeking to share enjoyment with other people by a lack of showing, bringing objects of interest to other people...a lack of social or emotional reciprocity.* The furniture and walls of definition are familiar and comforting. *Encompassing preoccupation with patterns of interest... abnormal in either intensity or focus... inflexible adherence to specific, nonfunctional routines or rituals....* And the part that makes me feel redeemed, because I am a smart animal: *no clinically significant delay in cognitive development ...adaptive behavior or curiosity about the environment....*

For some of us, the listed features have become a kind of penance of memory, a litany of things real about us or those we love, a wailing wall that receives our notes of isolation, of contradiction, of sometimes reluctant specialty; it shades us from the weather of uncertainty and offers us the shelter of classification. Like most other definitions of being, it houses a small few, denying membership to many, and perhaps it is rightly so, as few on the outside would seek to call it home. I can scan the familiar page and see the lines as furniture in a place I visit often in my mind.

The comfortable familiarity that lies within the lines of the page, within the diagnosis, within the label, within the ink of distinction, is almost seductive. We define to apprehend. We define to tame. We define the fineness of animal unpredictability and trade it for the confinement of brackets and bars, the static of staying. We make these unwieldy things out of our control become unfinished, the static of staying more peaceful to us than the call of the wild.

What strikes me after learning about differences and diagnoses for many years is that a clear and persistent pattern of a way of being is necessary for a diagnosis: enough people must have a certain obvious and readily identifiable set of features about them to be recognized as belonging in a category of difference. This means that a significant number of people in the population must follow this pattern, and enough of those must have presented themselves to the identifiers of patterns in our culture for their way of being to be recognized. This begs the question of whether or not something so prevalent, so persistent can be abnormal or if it is just a normal way of being, or, perhaps, an evolutionary trend.

Because of this I think the Diagnostic and Statistical Manual that is now used to diagnose our pathologies with should not be the enormous tome it has become. It would include only one entry: a diagnosis for debilitating normality, for this is truly pathological. Perhaps it would read like this:

Qualitative impairment in social interaction, as manifested by marked impairments in the use of multiple nonverbal behaviors facial expression, body postures, and gestures, that expose oddness; A lack of spontaneous seeking to share oddness (e.g. by a lack of showing, bringing, or pointing out objects of interest that are strange); A lack of social or emotional reciprocity in regard to difference; Encompassing preoccupation with one or more restricted patterns of interest that is abnormal in either intensity or focus (e.g. a debilitating focus on being "like everyone else") ; Apparently inflexible adherence to specific, nonfunctional routines or rituals (e.g. obsessive or compulsive patterns of behavior believed to make one more "like everyone else".) The disturbance causes clinically significant impairments in social, occupational, or other areas of functioning (e.g. one's feelings of connection and self-fulfillment); There is no clinically significant delay in cognitive development or in the development of age-appropriate self-help skills, adaptive behavior and curiosity about the environment in childhood…

I believe diagnoses should come to be seen as descriptions, and the gifts of a way of being should be included in these descriptions. Disability is, in my definition, a state in which suffering has no context, in which suffering and struggle have no cultural meaning. As we pathologize and intereriorize certain ways of being, maybe we are trying to take suffering away; after all freakishness lies in visibility. No one would pay to see Brain Tumor Woman, or Macular Degeneration Man. We have to be able to readily perceive and identify strangeness on the surface. But I think such obvious freakishness – which ultimately exists in us all – has to be worn on the sleeve to give it meaning. Its meaning must come from being shared.

As a person who has been successful as a freak, I know that if everything goes right, I may be out of a job if everyone else sees these things the same way I do. I feel like the man in the story circus owner and manager John Robinson tells to sum up circus life in the 1860s: One morning a remarkable specimen of young man came to the circus grounds looking for a job. His hair was at least a foot and a half long, and his hair and beard looked like a haystack after a cyclone. He was hired on the spot as a wild man; they even gave him a dollar to bind the contract. They told him to report for work that afternoon. At around one o'clock, the man came back, ready for work. He had spent his dollar at the barber, getting cleaned up for the show. The freak had become anyone, and everyone.

Novelist Philip Roth, speaking perhaps inadvertently to the truth of the normal freaks that surround us, wrote that the "American writer…has his hands full in trying to understand, and then describe, and then make *credible* much of American reality…it is even a kind of embarrassment to one's own meager imagination. The actuality is continually outdoing our talents, and the culture tosses up figures almost daily that are the envy of every novelist."

And so we see books like *Skinny Women are Evil: Notes of a Big Girl in a Small-Minded World; She's Not There: A Life in Two Genders; The Leg and I: A Rollicking Autobiography of an Amputee;* and *Hey! Ho! It's the White Negro!* And we can't leave out *How to Become a Schizophrenic*; *Old Age: It's Cause and Prevention*; *My Duodenal Ulcer and I*; and the ubiquitous *My Prostate and Me.*

Eighty-one percent of the population, seeing titles such as these each day and knowing that they, too, all qualify as "qualitatively different" from the *seemingly* normal people around them, feel they have a book inside them. The persistent attraction toward perceived freakishness (and its marketability) is reflected in the fact that 28% of those who "have a book in them" would write on personal development and 27% would write biography. Many people actually follow through: six million people have written a manuscript that is currently making the rounds.

"The freakish is no longer a private zone," Susan Sontag has said encouragingly. "Hobbesian man roams the streets quite visible, with glitter in his hair." But it is important to finally understand that we seek the freakish not because we are sick or maladjusted, and not because the freakish is so far *outside* our experience, but because it is *inside* us, every one. I am entertained by anecdotes of the freakish, of the monstrous, of the bizarre, like any reader, like any human being, because I see myself there. People forget that the word "entertainment" comes from the Latin *inter* (among) and *tenere* (to hold). An audience needs to feel like they identify with what they see if they are to become truly engrossed.

And yet, of all the books ever published (since 1776, 22 million titles have been published; there are about 2.8 million books in print, and about 120,000 titles are published each year) I couldn't find any that address the fact that *no one* is normal, that were are all passing. Of the six large publishers (in New York), 3,000 -4,000 medium-sized publishers, 86,000 small/self-publishers and more than 10,000 non-profit publishers, no one that I could discern is stating this obvious fact and publishing about it. And although readers spend roughly $26.9 billion annually on books, they aren't demanding books that speak more broadly to what they must all secretly know is true. I'm waiting. I think we're all waiting.

In the meantime, here are some of the great books on freaks I used in researching this work, and ones I enjoyed and recommend: Robert Bogdan's *Freak Show: Presenting Human Oddities for Amusement and Profit* (Univeristy of Chicago Press, 1990); Jan Bondeson's *A Cabinet of Medical Curiosities* (W.W. Norton & Company, 1999); Lennard J. Davis' *The Disability Studies Reader* (Routledge, 1977); Martin Howard's *Victorian Grotesque: An Illustrated Excursion into Medical Curiosities, Freaks, and Abnormalities, Principally of the Victorian Age* (Jupiter Books, 1977); Jack Hunter's *Freak Babylon* (Glitter Books, 2005); Daniel P. Mannix's *Freaks: We Who are Not Like Others* (Re/Search Publications, 2000); Michael Michell's *Monsters: Human Freaks in America's Gilded Age: The Photographs of Charles Issenmann* (Ecw Press, 2002); A. W. Stencell's *Seeing is Believing: America's Side Shows* (Ecw Press, 2002) and Andre Stulman Dennett's *Weird and*

Wonderful: The Dime Museum in America (New York University Press, 1997).

I hope you have enjoyed this one, too.

Made in the USA
Coppell, TX
31 January 2021

49255051R00135